WILLIAM WALLACE

WILLIAM WALLACE

ANDREW FISHER

JOHN DONALD PUBLISHERS LTD
EDINBURGH

ISBN 0 85976 154 1

Reprinted 1988
Reprinted 1992
Reprinted 1994
Reprinted 1995 (twice)
Reprinted 1996 (twice)
Reprinted 1997

Phototypesetting by Print Origination, Liverpool.
Printed in Great Britain by J. W. Arrowsmith Ltd.,
Bristol

Acknowledgements

I am indebted to Dr. Norman Macdougall of the University of St. Andrews for his courteous help and advice. The staff of the Carlisle branch of Cumbria County Library and of Cumbria Records Office, Carlisle have always been patient and cheerful when faced by requests for texts over a lengthy period. John Tuckwell of John Donald Publishers has, with gentle persistence, encouraged me to complete the book. My family has been no less encouraging. I am grateful to all. I owe a particular debt to Professor G.W.S. Barrow, whom I have never met. No one who aspires to know the period of the war between Scotland and England can hope to do so without reference to his work. If I differ from him about the relationship of Wallace to Wishart and the Stewart, I do so with respect.

Where I have sinned, I have done so without help from the above!

The cover illustration is taken from a drawing by James Proudfoot of the Battle of Stirling Bridge and is reproduced by kind permission of Stirling District Council. Readers may incidentally care to visit the National Wallace Monument between Stirling and Bridge of Allan, which is open from February to October inclusive.

Contents

Introduction

William Wallace was born into a Scotland long at peace with its southern neighbour and, since the battle of Largs and the treaty of Perth, rid of the fear of invasion from Norway. His family, though landed and titled and like its feudal superiors, the Stewarts, established in Scotland for over a century, was not noble. Such education as he received was rudimentary, distinguished only by that love of liberty which he retained to the end of his life. Before his invasion of the north of England in late 1297, he had never, as far as we are aware, left Scotland. His contacts were unexceptional, restricted by the rigidly hierarchical nature of the society in which he lived. A younger son, he had few prospects and an uncertain future.

He was thus in no way prepared, by birth, education, or training, for a role of any consequence in the history of his native land. Yet when the ambition of Edward I combined with the weakness of John Balliol to usher in that conflict which we choose to call the Scottish War of Independence, Wallace was to rise within a year to an eminence and reputation, in Europe as in Scotland, which none could have foreseen. He led and directed the resistance to Edward, broke the sequence of English successes in the field, maintained the cause of John Balliol, restored his country to its rightful place in the councils of Europe, and where others, ostensibly his betters, yielded and collaborated, set an example of constancy and perseverance. Even his death was seen as a victory. He became and remained an inspiration to both singer and poet. Wallace was by any standards a remarkable man.

But if undoubtedly a hero, he was not perfect. There is to Wallace not merely a dark but an unknown side. In an age of brutality, he was brutal. He was no less cruel than those against whom he fought. He repaid the sack of Berwick with the harrying of Northumberland. To achieve his ends, he turned violently on any, Scots or English, who stood in his way. The crimes with which he would be charged by Edward's justices in 1305 were not wholly fabrications; Wallace himself at his trial, far from seeking to deny or excuse them, gloried in what he had done. Posterity, however, as it has done in the case of his contemporary, Robert Bruce, has tended to look away from his flaws as if afraid of the truth. Wallace was, simply, a

1

man of his time with all that means; our recognition of the fact does not detract from his stature. More significant, and more harmful to the memory of Wallace, is the manner in which our lamentable ignorance of his life before 1297 and of the period between the defeat at Falkirk and his death seven years later has led us to neglect a number of crucial questions connected with him. The result is that we have made something of a one-dimensional figure of a man who cannot have been other than complicated. Of such questions three in particular present themselves for our consideration. First, how could a man untutored in the art of war and without experience in its practice emerge with such authority and ability as a military leader in the early months of 1297? Second, on the basis of the admittedly meagre information available to us, what role can we allocate to Wallace after Falkirk which fits our knowledge of his character, temperament, and talents? Third, given that the traditional link between Wallace's execution in August 1305 and Bruce's murder of Comyn in February 1306 and his subsequent rebellion is now discredited, what was the relationship between Wallace and Bruce?

It is not to be expected that the answer to these questions is to be discovered in contemporary sources. Wallace is at best a shadowy figure and likely to remain so. But that has not prevented criticism of his decision to fight at Falkirk or the general agreement that his defeat there inevitably brought in its train his resignation as Guardian. It has not prevented an unflattering comparison of him with Andrew Murray, or, more seriously, a view of him which is condescending and therefore detrimental. Wallace deserves better of us. It is too much to see in him one who, as it were, sprang forth ready-made in 1297, remained fixed and unalterable over a period of some eight years, learned and forgot nothing, was never tempted to despair, never profited from the study of the political manoeuvres of his Scottish associates, never deviated from a pre-ordained path. Wallace was not such a man. Much of what we believe of him is interpretation, not fact. That is understandable given our ignorance. But if we accept that we do not know, and cannot know, the whole story of William Wallace, we can look at him again and in offering an answer to our questions, come closer to an authentic picture of the first and most enduring hero of Scottish nationalism.

Map 1. Scotland in the Early Years of the War with England, 1297-1305.

CHAPTER 1

The Silent Years

When in 1124 David I succeeded his brother, Alexander I, as king of Scotland, he was already firmly committed to the introduction into his new kingdom of the Anglo-Norman system of government.[1] Raised at the English court from the age of eight,[2] he had studied the principles and the practice of that system at first hand, especially with the encouragement of his brother-in-law, Henry I. Through the administration of his own considerable estates in England[3] and, later, of those parts of Lothian ceded to him by Alexander, he had gained further and more personal experience. He thus brought with him as king not merely a philosophy of government but the first of those men from England who would help him rule Scotland on the Anglo-Norman model.[4] He began to surround himself with the acquaintances of his youth, ambitious, thrusting adventurers, men determined upon success and its corollary, the acquisition of land. To the reign of David I we may trace the appearance in Scotland of many of the great names of the country's history, among them Bruce, Balliol, and Comyn. Of these particular families, the first two would in time themselves produce kings of Scotland, while the third, unlike them almost entirely forgotten today, may have been prevented from the achievement of monarchy by the precipitate and murderous action of the most famous of the Bruces.

In or about the year 1136, as part of the process of creating in Scotland what would become a new aristocracy, David took into his service as 'dapifer' or steward of the household a certain Walter, the third son of Alan Fitzalan and his wife Avelina.[5] It was a position of undoubted trust and responsiblity that the king had offered Walter, although its holder did not at that time rank quite among the highest officers of state. Walter's family had been hereditary stewards to the lords of Dol in eastern Brittany since the middle of the eleventh century. Indeed, his eldest brother, Jordan, returned to Dol from England, where the family had settled in the early years of the reign of Henry I, to carry on the established tradition. We do not know the circumstances in which David the future king of Scotland and Walter his future steward first met. It may have been as early as 1114 when they, like Alexander I, campaigned in Wales under Henry I. Whatever the occasion of their meeting, David did not forget the other

4

man. As a younger son, Walter had few prospects of advancement as long as he remained in England, and it is likely therefore that he accepted David's offer of employment with both alacrity and gratitude. The ability to recognise and, equally important, to act upon an opportunity was, after all, an inherited characteristic. Walter's father, Alan, had been a close associate of William the Conqueror's youngest son when the latter's route to the throne of England had seemed blocked. But when Henry took advantage of the unexpected death of his brother, William II, in August 1100, to make himself king, he did not neglect his old friend. Alan, it has been written, 'benefited substantially, not to say spectactularly, after Henry had acquired the English throne'.[6]

In keeping with his new dignity as steward, Walter Fitzalan was granted by David and his grandson and immediate heir, Malcolm IV, extensive holdings in Renfrew, Ayrshire, and Lothian.[7] In marriage he took Eschina de Londres, and their son, Alan, succeeded upon Walter's death in 1177 to what had by now become a hereditary office. Alan's son, Walter II, followed his father in office in 1204 with the more impressive-sounding title of 'seneschallus'. It was this Walter who was the first to be known as 'Steward of Scotland'. Yet another Walter, the sixth in the line introduced into Scotland by David I in 1136, married in 1316 Marjorie Bruce, daughter of Robert I. Through this union the Stewarts became the ruling house of Scotland in 1371 when the son of Walter and Marjorie became king as Robert II, and they were later, in the person of James VI and I, to mount the throne of England.

The appointment of a steward by David I in 1136 was thus of immense significance for the history of Scotland. It resulted also in the arrival in the country of another family which, through the career of one man, was to become more celebrated in the popular imagination than the Stewarts themselves. We have seen that Walter Fitzalan decided to leave England at the invitation of David I because he was frustrated in his ambitions. His brother, William II Fitzalan, had been more fortunate. He had achieved a position of some standing in England, not least in Shropshire, where he was lord of Oswestry. Among those listed as owing him service in 1166 was one Richard Wallace.[8] At an unknown date Richard elected to follow Walter Fitzalan to Scotland, and as the other had profited from the move to the northern kingdom, so did Richard, although on a lesser scale. It is from this Richard Wallace or le Waleis, that is the Welshman, that William the Guardian of Scotland is generally held to be descended.[9] The name of Richard Wallace is found as a witness to a charter granted in 1174 by Walter I Stewart to the abbey of Paisley. Towards the end of the next century, in the first years of the War of Independence with England, the names of Wallace and Stewart were once again to be linked. If in that context the former is better and with more reason remembered, it remained until 1297 obscure in comparison to that of its feudal superior.

Richard Wallace flourished under Walter I, and it is possible that he survived as late as the time of Walter II. He was granted lands in Kyle, and it is tempting to include among these Riccarton, as commemorating his name. Of Richard and the other early members of the Wallace family we know little other than through their relationship with the Stewarts.[10] The family was unremarkable and, it may reasonably be assumed, would have remained so but for the War of Independence. Before that war, it would seem that no event occurred involving the family, no deed was done by any of its members, sufficient to attract the attention of contemporaries. If unremarkable, the family was, however, widespread, a fact to which it will be necessary to return to explain at least one aspect of the career of William the Guardian.

It is likely that, as tradition has long had it, William, Richard Wallace's descendant, was born at Elderslie, near Paisley. The year of his birth has never been satisfactorily established. A great deal of effort has been spent, much of it on the basis of contradictory information supplied by his celebrated if unreliable biographer, to settle the question.[11] If it is futile to add to that effort, we shall not be far wrong if we content ourselves with the observation that William was still a young man when he first made his name in 1297. The nature of what might be termed his 'historical' life was such that only a man in his prime would be capable of living it. An outline of the details, sparse enough in themselves, serves to prove the point. Between 1297 and his death in 1305 William is known to have raised a rebellion against the English who occupied his country, defeated Surrey and killed Cressingham at Stirling, overcome the subsequent loss of the formidable and inspirational Murray, cleared Scotland of effective English troops, led an army on a destructive campaign in winter through the northern counties of England, returned to Scotland to carry on the government in the face of the doubts, not to say the opposition, of the native nobility, maintained an army in being and trained it, fought against and almost defeated the hitherto invincible Edward I at Falkirk, escaped that monarch, travelled to the Continent, certainly to France, where he survived a period of imprisonment, moved on to Rome and perhaps further still, made his way back to Scotland in hazardous conditions, and for almost five years more continued either openly or from hiding the struggle against the superior and relentless enemy into whose possession he was ultimately betrayed. We need none of the embroidery in which

Blind Harry indulged to draw the obvious conclusion. It is difficult to see how the physical strength without which he could have done little of this, not to mention the robustness of mind necessary to sustain him in the face of adversity, could have been found in one who was not young.

A comparison with part of the career of Robert Bruce may help to underline the above argument. When in February 1306 Bruce murdered his enemy and rival, John Comyn of Badenoch, in Dumfries, he was forced not long afterwards to emulate William and go into hiding to escape the vengeance of Edward I.[12] Fortunately for Bruce, he was spared the years of pursuit suffered by William, for Edward was dead at Burgh-by-Sands in July of the following year and Edward II, although determined to retain Scotland, lacked his father's obsessive drive. Bruce's adventures are well enough recorded to make clear the strains under which he laboured while a fugitive from the first Edward's justice. At the time of the murder of Comyn, Bruce was five months short of his thirty-second birthday.

William's relationship with Andrew Murray[13] appears to support the view that in 1297 he was in his prime, perhaps of an age with Bruce. Murray was himself a young man when he and William joined forces, and he came of a family which was a major vassal of the Scottish Crown. He and William had, it would appear, nothing in common, the one the heir to a great and honourable inheritance, his new colleague at worst an outlaw. Yet, from the evidence available to us, we can see that each took at once to the other. Their alliance, however weighted,[14] was to prove of inestimable value to the Scottish cause. It could hardly have come about without trust. That trust, and their relationship as a whole, is more easily explained if we accept that they were of the same generation. The attributes which they shared and which united them were, too, those of the young. They did not hesitate or prevaricate where their elders had faltered with such disastrous consequences for Scotland. They did not respect nor were they overawed by reputation. The slow but impressive parade of the English army before Stirling did not break their resolve. Given an opportunity by the incompetence of Surrey and Cressingham, they fought and were right to do so. The decision to attack the English army, despite the great power it had demonstrated in previous encounters with the Scots, surely belonged to young men, as did the victory which resulted.

If contemporary records are silent on the matter of William's age at the time of his prominence and we are denied whatever information Blind Harry had, ignorance has not deterred all of William's biographers. A standardised and widely popular account of his early life has long been available that combines what little fact we do have with the offerings of Blind Harry. According to the version which thus emerges,[15] William was the son of Sir Malcolm Wallace of Elderslie, the great-great-grandson of Richard Wallace, and his wife, variously Margaret or Jean, the daughter of Sir Reginald Crawford of Crosbie, hereditary sheriff of Ayr. The most famous member of the Wallace family was neither an only child, nor the first born to his parents. Named among his brothers are John and Malcolm. Blind Harry alone credits him with two sisters. William is said to have been educated by his uncle, a priest, at Dunipace, and subsequently by a second uncle who was also a priest, at Dundee. We are told that while a student at Dunipace he was taught by his uncle an abiding love of liberty, usually quoted in the Latin couplet:

> Dico te verbum, libertas optima rerum;
> Nunquam servili sub nexu vivito, fili.[16]

During his sojourn at Dundee, he is said to have made the acquaintance of John Blair, a Benedictine monk. Blair, either at this time or later, left the contemplative life, and became William's chaplain, constantly at his side in the great struggle to which William dedicated himself. In his retirement at Dunfermline, where he died, Blair wrote a life of William on which Blind Harry, with due acknowledgement, drew. If we believe the traditional account, William was, by the standards of the time and given his origins, well educated. Thus he was familiar with French as well as Latin. Since he was a younger son, he was, we are left to assume, intended for the priesthood, following in the steps of the uncles to whom he owed his education. What appears to have been an uneventful and happy life, not to say an idyllic one, was interrupted by the machinations of the ruthless and evil Edward I.

We should not too readily dismiss this popular version of William's early life. We know little enough of him before 1297 to dare entirely to disregard what has over the years become, for many, not legend but fact. If Blind Harry used the work of John Blair, now lost, who is to say that he did not have other sources, also lost to us? But what has come down to us from Blind Harry in the standard version does not answer the fundamental question of the transformation of the unknown younger son into the colossal figure of 1297. It has the advantage, however, that it leads quite naturally to what might be called the romantic and cataclysmic view of the reason for William's first recorded assault upon the English, in 1297. William, we are to understand, could only have been forced out of the quiet and placid life he had known by some single violent act or by personal tragedy or, better still, by a combination of the two. In this context, the intervention of Edward I in the internal affairs of the kingdom of Scotland must, of course, provide the setting, the murder by the English sheriff of

Lanark, the unspeakable William Heselrig, of William' wife or mistress, Marion Braidfute, heiress of Lamington, the occasion. This explanation of the supposed conversion from the student of theology to the practitioner of warfare appears to contain a contradiction within itself. The relationship with Marion Braidfute, whether that of husband or lover, is not what one would expect of a man bent, we have already been led to believe, on the life of a priest. The hot-blooded, savage murder of Heselrig, with no thought given to the consequences, is, on the other hand, exactly the reaction of the young man William is generally perceived to have been in 1297.

The legend of Marion Braidfute, with its accompanying account of William's life, persists. But even if based on truth, it is not enough. It does not address an absorbing question: the origins of William's military skill. Nothing in the words of Blind Harry or in those who follow him prepares us for the genius of 1297-1298. How, then, are we to explain that genius? There would appear to be three possible answers. The first is that, unknown to us, he had before 1297 served an apprenticeship as a soldier. It follows from this that he had left Scotland to fight, for no opportunity was to be found in his homeland. Whatever adventures he conjures up for William, not even Blind Harry hints at such a passage in William's life before 1297. Yet can we ignore this possibility? What better career existed for a younger, landless son than that of a soldier, the more so if the young man was, as later events were to show, exceptionally equipped for the role? If William did indeed seek employment as a soldier and therefore went abroad, both Wales and France suggest themselves as areas to which he might have directed his steps in, for example, 1293-4. In both countries William's later enemy, Edward I, was engaged. It is an intriguing thought, but one incapable of proof, that William might have already served in a campaign in which the English king was involved. It is even more intriguing to think, but just as incapable of proof, that he, like more than one of his fellow-countrymen, fought not against but with Edward.

If William was a soldier, his involvement in the war with England prior to 1297 must be considered. While the possibility cannot be ignored, it seems unlikely that his involvement would have escaped the attention of later writers, whether Scottish or English. For the former, it would underline his total commitment to the Scottish cause, for the latter it would surely be used as an indication that his treason was of longer standing than is usually accepted. Each school of thought would be confirmed in its prejudice and not fail to give it expression.

The second answer, which, like the first, helps to fill part of the gap in our knowledge of his life, is that he learned something of the skill of a soldier while an outlaw. William the outlaw is, of course, a familiar and

appealing theme.[17] Blind Harry could not resist it. There is about
William's adventures, in the form they are transmitted to us by Harry, the
mark of the outlaw: the bravado, the challenges given and taken, the
impudence, the insults, the exceptional talent with the bow, the careless-
ness of death, the protection of and by the poor, above all, the heroic
stature in the face of great odds. Thus, William slays the son of Selby, the
English constable of Dundee,[18] as, historically, he slew Heselrig, as an
affront to a superior and detested enemy. The outlaw does not hide from
the enemy but instead seeks him out. All this we can recognise as
traditional outlaw lore. But it has a basic flaw. As will be seen, William was
a careful, even painstaking man. Far from seeking out the enemy, he
prepared to meet him on William's own terms. Neither at Stirling nor
Falkirk did William seek battle.

We do not know whether William was truly an outlaw before the murder
of Heselrig. That same younger, landless son who might have become a
soldier might, equally, have turned to a life of crime. The two indeed are
not exclusive. The military catastrophe of 1296 must have forced many
Scots into crime. If William was an outlaw, his deeds may well have been
far from heroic. There exists one tantalising piece of evidence from the year
1296. The records of the time tell us that on 8 August: 'Matthew of York,
accused by Cristiana of St. John, of robbery, viz. on Thursday next before
St. Botulph's Day, he came to her house at Perth in company of a thief, one
William le Waleys, and there by force took her goods and chattels viz. beer,
to the value of 3s., replies that he is a clerk and not bound to answer. The
jury finds the charge proved, and he is adjudged to penitence'.[19] At the
time of this entry, Balliol had already been deposed and Scotland was an
occupied country. Perhaps the William Wallace who robbed the unfortunate Cristiana in Perth, a favourite stamping-ground of the Guardian, had
fought under Balliol and was now living as best he could. He was, at least,
clever enough not to be caught, unlike his colleague, Matthew.

The outlaw depends for his survival not merely upon his wits and his
skill but upon the sympathy and protection of those among whom he lives.
Such sympathy and the protection it brings have to be earned, and it is
common therefore to find the outlaw the friend and defender of the poor.
The William Wallace of history has no such pedigree. His cause was a
different one. Yet he could not have stayed out of the hands of the English
without the goodwill of many. His murder of Heselrig made him an
outlaw, whether or not he had been one under the law of Scotland. That
murder was accomplished, as we shall see, with a band of followers. Where
had he gathered this force? His personal magnetism would no doubt attract
men to him, as it did to the end of his life. Deeds of which we are ignorant

would add to his admirers. The disaffected, the disenchanted, those already feeling the weight of English oppression, would swell the ranks of those about him.

There was, however, another source on which Wallace could draw both before and during 1297: the Wallace family itself. The extent of the Wallace holdings before the death of Walter II Stewart has been shown by Barrow.[20] These, far from being limited to the west of Scotland where Richard settled and where William was born, stretched across the centre of the country, into the east and north into Moray.[21] They breach the barriers, that is, of region, language, and culture. They guaranteed an inheritance of relationships and connections to the descendants of Richard Wallace. When William came to his great endeavour, did he call upon that inheritance? Did he later, hunted by the English and their Scottish collaborators, use that inheritance in another and no less critical situation? Was he hidden from pursuers in the employ of the English king as once, perhaps, he had been helped while an outlaw before the war? It is evident that he could not have survived in the earlier as in the later part of his career had there not been an immense sympathy for him wherever he went. If, after 1297, he benefited from his exploits against the hated English, it is not unreasonable to argue that he could already rely upon the members of his own widely scattered family. His brother John, executed in London, his older brother Malcolm, who inherited Elderslie, they alone cannot represent the true contribution of the Wallace family to William's work.[22]

The theory of William the outlaw, however attractive, fails in one significant area to answer our question. It is not the way of the outlaw to fight pitched battles, least of all on the scale of Stirling and Falkirk. The outlaw is adept at the ambush, at the tactic of hit and run. William, like Murray, began in this style and returned to it after Falkirk. By that time he had already demonstrated an ability to organise and use large armies for which the life of an outlaw is neither explanation nor preparation. We know of no one in his company either before or at the time of the murder of Heselrig from whom he could have learned the necessary skills. The Scottish leaders with whom he associated after the murder, even if we put aside their suspicion and distrust of him, had no record of proven success in the field and were, on the contrary, wholly discredited.

We are thus forced back on the third and most obvious explanation of William's military genius: that he was born with it. The war with England provided an arena for a man possessed of such enormous talent, and not merely in the profession of arms, as would have guaranteed him success in whatever direction he cared to employ it. If the claim seems extravagant, one need only look at the challenge he faced as Guardian and the manner in which he dealt with it. The soldier became the governor and assumed the latter role with the same exceptional competence as he had the former. But in neither function could he have achieved what he did if he had been the one-dimensional figure with which we are accustomed to deal. If his talent as a soldier was innate, we have, in order to explain what he accomplished, to see him in a new light. In this connection it is instructive to turn to the work of an authority on the subject of war. Clausewitz writes: 'If we then ask what sort of mind is likeliest to display the qualities of military genius, experience and observation will both tell us that it is the inquiring rather than the creative mind, the comprehensive rather than the specialized approach, the calm rather than the excitable head to which in war we would choose to entrust the fate of our brothers and children and the safety and honour of our country'.[23] Machiavelli is less ready that Clausewitz to speak of genius. He contents himself with listing general rules of military discipline.[24] In them and what follows we find that other characteristic which in Wallace balances the view of Clausewitz. Machiavelli states, firstly, that 'good commanders never come to an engagement unless they are compelled to by absolute necessity, or occasion calls for it'.[25] He then goes on to deal, in closing, with the qualifications which distinguish the general.[26] Whatever skill the general has, he will not prosper 'unless he has abilities to strike out something new of his own occasionally. For no man ever excelled in his profession who could not do that, and if a ready and quick invention is necessary and honourable in any profession, it must certainly be so in the art of war above all others. Thus we see how any invention or new expedient, trifling though it may be, is celebrated by historians'.

We cannot be sure that the exploits of Wallace came to the attention of either Clausewitz or Machiavelli. He was perhaps too slight a figure on the scale on which they worked. Yet we cannot ignore the fact that in their writings we read of Wallace if not by name then through the attributes which they seek in the soldier and especially in the comander. Both were protagonists of the professional soldier, and their study of what was for them an art was exhaustive. While we can recognise in Machiavelli's words that particular feeling for improvisation which was so important in his career, it is in Clausewitz that we come closer to what Wallace was as a soldier. The qualities to which Clausewitz refers are not those with which tradition has endowed William; they are too clinical, too cold even, for that William. We are accustomed to thinking of him as a man of passion, driven forward against the English by his surpassing patriotism, the leader of an undisciplined army swept forward whatever the odds. There is, undeniably, something of that in the Wallace of history. It may have been there at

Lanark. If it was, it disappeared in the new and more difficult circumstances in which he found himself. It is then that we see the William who came so near to the ideal of which Clausewitz wrote. We need not dispense with the Wallace of tradition, burning with anger, brutal, unforgiving. He was all of that. But he had, too, a passion for success, for without that his country could not be free. He came to the war with England without the prejudices and preconceptions which his feudal superiors so frequently and wantonly manifested. He had to learn, and to learn he had to enquire. He was not bound by sectional interests, as were those superiors; his was the wider, if simpler, view. He approached battle in a rational, careful way and was not driven to it by the unmanageable bloodlust which had so inflamed Scottish leaders before him that they charged to defeat.

In William Wallace we are dealing with a man unique in his time and place. Scotland produced no one comparable in the War of Independence. Those who came before him taught him by default, those after learned from him the vital lessons which won the war. We can only wonder that, without formal training, lacking, as far as we are aware, reputation either inherited or earned, he emerged from obscurity so complete a soldier. It is a chastening thought that without war he would have remained unknown or at best, if he was indeed an outlaw under Scottish law, a footnote in history. That likelihood disappeared when the death of Alexander III of Scotland set in train the events which brought Wallace so memorably into the consciousness of his countrymen, from which he has never been displaced.

NOTES

1. For general reading on the reign of David I, see Ritchie: *The Normans in Scotland*, 1953; Barrow: *The Kingdom of the Scots*, 1973; Barrow: *The Anglo-Norman Era in Scottish History*, 1980; Barrow: *Feudal Britain, the Completion of the Medieval Kingdoms, 1066-1314*, 1956; all *passim*. Dickinson: *Scotland from the Earliest Times to 1603*, 1962, esp. chaps. 9, 11, 13, 15. On particular aspects of the reign, Burleigh: *A Church History of Scotland*, 1960; Lawrie (ed.): *Early Scottish Charters prior to 1153*, 1905; Anderson (coll. & trans.): *Early Sources of Scottish History, 500-1286*, 1922; Barrow: *Scottish Rulers and the religious orders*, R.H.S., 5th. series, iii, 1953, 77-100.

2. Of this period William of Malmesbury wrote: 'He [David] had rubbed off all tarnish of Scottish barbarity through being polished from his boyhood by intercourse and friendship with us'. (q. Cowan: 'Myth and Identity in Early Medieval Scotland', *S.H.R.* LXIII, 2, no. 176, October 1984, 131).

3. Of these he gained through his marriage to Matilda, the daughter and heiress of Waltheof, executed for treason under William I, the earldom of Northampton and the Honour of Huntingdon, which proved fertile recruiting grounds for David.

4. Barrow: *Anglo-Norman Era,* and Ritchie: *The Normans in Scotland, passim;* Brown: 'The Origin of the House of Stewart', *S.H.R.,* xxiv, 1927. J.G. Wilson: 'Walter Fitzalan, first hereditary high Steward of Scotland', *Scot Geneal.* XXIIX, 1982, 84–85.

5. Barrow: *Anglo-Norman Era,* 14.

6. Barrow: *Anglo-Norman Era,* 13.

7. Brown: *Origin,* 265-279; Barrow: *Kingdom,* chap. 12.

8. Kightly: *Folk Heroes of Britain,* 1982, 157; Barrow: *Anglo-Norman Era,* 66.

9. *D.N.B.,* 563; Kightly, 157. The family name, although translated as meaning 'Welsh' (man), is unlikely to refer to Welsh origins but rather to the border region. Reaney: *A Dictionary of British Surnames,* 1976, 369.

10. Barrow: *Kingdom of the Scots* advances the interesting theory, 352-3, that the Wallace and the Ness families were one and the same.

11. The article in *D.N.B.* gives some idea of the problems posed by Blind Harry in this regard.

12. McNair Scott: *Robert the Bruce King of Scots,* 1982, chap. 8; Barrow: *Robert Bruce and the Community of the Realm of Scotland,* 1976, chaps. 9 & 10. An interesting commentary on the view of Wallace found in Barrow can be seen in A.A.M. Duncan's review of the book in *S.H.R.* vol. XLV, 2, Oct. 1966, 184-193. In particular Duncan states (193) that Barrow is 'Extraordinarily reluctant to see him [Wallace] as a free agent'. See also Barron: *The Scottish War of Independence,* 1934, chaps. 21-24.

13. Barron: chaps. 7 & 8 contains what is perhaps the most famous assessment of that relationship.

14. See Barron, chaps. 7 & 8 for the weighting in favour of Murray. It reflects no doubt the need for a balance to the traditional view of Wallace but errs in the direction of according to Murray a pre-eminence which, in the light of his early death, cannot adequately be tested against events.

15. An example of such an account is to be found in, among others, Murison: *Sir William Wallace,* with its heavy reliance on Blind Harry. As a corrective see the more restrained versions offered in more recent works – Murison's work was published in 1898 – e.g. Kightly, 156-8; Barrow: *Robert Bruce,* 109-110.

16. *D.N.B.,* 564.

17. Keen: *The Outlaws of Medieval Legend,* 1961, chap, 64.

18. Blind Harry: First Book.

19. Bain (ed.): *Calendar of Documents,* ii, p. 191.

20. *Kingdom,* chap. 12.

21. *Ibid.*

22. *D.N.B.,* 563.

23. Clausewitz: *On War,* ed. Howard & Paret, 1984, 112.

24. Machiavelli: *The Art of War,* trans. Farneworth, 1965, 202-204.

25. *Ibid.,* 203-204.

26. *Ibid.,* 205-206.

CHAPTER 2

The Time of Defeat, 1296-1297

The medieval mind was much obsessed by the concept of the Day of Judgement. All were agreed that there would come a time when an accounting would be called for. In Scotland one date set aside for what, according to the lives they had led on earth, some feared and others welcomed, was 18 March 1286, in the thirty-sixth year of the reign of Alexander III, descendant of David I.[1] From the beginning of this remarkable year, the weather, violent in the extreme, removed any lingering doubt that the people of Alexander's kingdom were right to anticipate some dread event. Only a foolish or brave man would disregard the omens. Such a man, as time would prove, was Alexander. On the day in question he met with his council in Edinburgh Castle. Among the items which occupied the attention of the king and his council was one relating to John Balliol, himself to play an important part in the events which followed upon the aftermath of the meeting.[2]

The work of the meeting finished, the king fed his councillors and plied them with wine. Nor did he stint himself with food or drink. As night drew on, the king's thoughts turned from matters of state to the attractions of his young wife, Yolande, daughter of the count of Dreux, whom he had married in October of the previous year. Alexander was then forty-four years of age and in robust health. He resolved that he would no longer be separated from his French wife. Yolande was at Kinghorn, a distance from Edinburgh of some twenty-two miles. Alexander was not deterred by the thought of a difficult journey made worse, not to say dangerous, by the darkness and the truly appalling weather. Perhaps the wine had affected his judgement. He referred with a joke to the universal despair which the year had engendered in his subjects. Dismissing the concerns voiced by the more timorous and superstitious among his councillors, he set out from Edinburgh that very evening for Kinghorn. Both at the ferry crossing at Dalmeny and, again, once over the Firth of Forth, he chose to disregard the urgent pleas of loyal servants and pressed on. With three esquires as companions and two local men acquired as guides, he rode impatiently along the coast road towards Kinghorn. Neither man nor nature could restrain him. The king had surely by this time forgotten what the humblest

15

of his subjects could have told him: that this was the Day of Judgement. And so it was to be, not only for Alexander but for the country over which he ruled. The disaster which so many had foretold now came about. In the darkness Alexander disappeared from the sight of his companions. The king who had so rashly ignored all the omens and scorned the elements fell to his death from the cliffs. We can imagine the consternation of those who had ridden with him, but nothing could be done that night. His body was found the next morning, his neck broken, on the shores of the Forth.[3] His subjects mourned his death and feared for the future.

Thus, in the pursuit of love, perished Alexander III, king of Scotland since the age of eight.[4] With him passed what in retrospect would seem an age of peace, prosperity and stability. Under him the nobles, many of them fractious, self-seeking and temperamentally violent, had become quiet, although, as became evident within a few years of his death, still possessed of the urge to fight when they believed their interests threatened. The country had been rendered safe from external pressures. The threat from Norway had been lifted by the victory of Largs in 1263 and the death on his way home of the defeated Hakon IV. The treaty of Perth three years later gave Alexander possession of the Western Isles and the Isle of Man in return for an initial payment and an annual rent.[5] The marriage of his daughter, Margaret, to Hakon's successor, Eric II, in 1281, and the birth of their child, another Margaret, drew the former enemies closer together. At the same time, England was seen neither as a threat nor as the enemy it had once been. Here, again, in this happy state of affairs, marriage played a part. With Edward I, brother of his first wife, Margaret, Alexander enjoyed an agreeable relationship. Ownership of the northern counties of England had ceased to be an issue likely to lead to war. The border line between the two countries had been settled in the reign of Alexander's father by the Treaty of York.[6] The question of English suzerainty over Scotland, like the border line so long a cause of friction, lay dormant if not forgotten by the English king.

Distance did not isolate Scotland from the rest of Europe. Where once the infiltration of Anglo-Norman families into Scotland under David I and Malcolm IV had ensured continued contact with the Continent, so, in the time of Alexander III, did trade, especially with those countries which lay on the North Sea.[7] Scotland, in 1286, therefore could look to the future with confidence. It was, it has been written, 'a country which was being gradually welded together, a country under law and order, with a strong government ably served by an efficient local administration'.[8]

The belief that the death of Alexander III on the night of 18-19 March 1286 marked the end of an era, that it occurred on what might truthfully be called a Day of Judgement, had not faded in the fifteenth century. It found expression in the words of Andrew Wyntoun:

Quhen Alysandyr our King was dede
That Scotland led in lure and le
Awaye was sons of ale and brede
Of wyne and wax, of gamyn and gle
Our gold was changed into lede
Chryst born into vyrgynte
Succour Scotland and remede
That stad is in perplexite.[9]

The transformation of Scotland after Alexander's death was not by any means, however, as abrupt or as complete as the plaintive, familiar words of Andrew Wyntoun might lead us to believe. The country survived, despite the opportunity Alexander's death offered, in the first instance, to the forces of disorder and disintegration already present within its borders and, in the second, to an astute and patient monarch in the kingdom to the south.

It is a measure of the basic achievement of Alexander's reign that the survival of Scotland was possible at all, for he had failed in one of the primary tests of a ruler's value. Alexander had not provided Scotland with a legitimate male heir capable of outliving him. He had twice married. Through his first marriage, in 1251 at the age of ten, to Margaret, daughter of Henry III of England, herself a year older, he had three children. The younger son, David, died in 1281 at the age of eight. The other son, named for his father, died in January 1284, a little past his twentieth birthday. The daughter, Margaret, who had become the wife of Eric II of Norway, died in 1283, at or soon after the birth of her daughter, also called Margaret. For ten years after the death of his wife, Alexander remained a widower. Whether he married Yolande of Dreux from love or through the need to produce an heir we do not know. Time, in any case, was not given him.

There was, however, an heir to the throne of Scotland in 1286. This was Margaret of Norway, Alexander's grand-daughter. The king had acted quickly – it might be said, ruthlessly, given the circumstances in which he found himself – upon the death of his son and heir in January 1284. Whatever grief he must have felt at the loss of the third and last surviving child of his marriage to Margaret of England, Alexander had not neglected the duty forced upon him to guarantee the succession. At Scone, therefore, no more than a week after the death of his namesake, Alexander caused his subjects, solemnly and in due form, to recognise his grand-daughter as his heir, failing other children born to him.[10] He thus rendered an exceptional service to his people. If in March 1286, at the time of her grandfather's death, Margaret of Norway was no more than three years old, in poor health, and a stranger to her new subjects, her claim to the throne was nevertheless upheld. An oath of loyalty to her was sworn and an undertaking given that her inheritance should be protected and kept in peace for her.[11]

That Margaret's claim to the throne was upheld indicates the general determination within Scotland that continuity should be paramount. The funeral of Alexander III and the subsequent gathering of the foremost in the land at Scone towards the end of April permitted discussion of policy for the period up to the coronation of the young queen, whenever that should be. The government of Scotland was therefore placed in the hands of six men, chosen by common consent as being representative of the nation as a whole.[12] They were termed '*custodes*', which today is customarily rendered as 'Guardians' rather than 'Wardens'. In one account of the events of 1286,[13] they are referred to specifically as 'custodes pacis' or 'Guardians of the peace', a more accurate description, at the beginning, of their primary and overriding function.

The peace of the kingdom was, indeed, soon under strain. Alexander III had hoped to ensure an undisturbed transfer of power by the oath of 1284, and that of 1286 had the same purpose. While there is no reason to doubt that those who gave their word on those occasions did so in sincerity, not all of them showed themselves capable of keeping it in the event. The centre of trouble was the south-west, inevitably, because of the relationship there of the Bruce and Balliol families. In what would today be called 'a preemptive strike', Robert Bruce the Competitor, lord of Annandale, and his son, Robert, earl of Carrick, seized the royal castles of Dumfries and Wigton as well as Buittle, which belonged to Balliol.[14] Further, at Turnberry, on 20 September 1286, the Bruces, father and son, joined with Angus Macdonald, Lord of the Isles, the earl of March, the earl of Menteith, James the Stewart, himself one of the Guardians, and other interested parties, in a pact, the meaning of which has been the source of much discussion.[15] Whatever the precise intention of the agreement or 'Band' of Turnberry, it and the disturbances which accompanied it, foreshadowed the more crucial readiness of the magnates to act as their interests dictated.[16] The strife in the south-west faded as quickly as it had appeared without further complications. The action of the Bruces was a warning, a rehearsal, of the inevitability of another Day of Judgement for Scotland.

The concept of the Guardianship stood the test of the troubles in the south-west, as did the authority of the six men who held the office during the crisis. It was to this office that William Wallace would later succeed on his own merits, and if we consider the names and titles of the first six Guardians, appointed after the death of Alexander III, we may begin to understand something of his achievement. Two bishops, William Fraser of St. Andrews and Robert Wishart of Glasgow, were named. With them served two of the earls of Scotland, Duncan of Fife and Alexander Comyn of Buchan, and two men drawn from the ranks of the barons, John Comyn of Badenoch and James the Stewart. Such men were, unlike William, of the classes accustomed to playing a part in the governing of Scotland. The choice of the six reflected both the realism of the nation and its politics. In essence, the groupings within the Guardians balanced the forces most capable of defending Scotland but, conversely, most likely, if unrestrained, to destroy it. Bruce and Balliol were the two most powerful families in the country; each family had its supporters among the Guardians. Of the bishops, Fraser favoured Balliol, Wishart Bruce. If the Comyns held to the former, James the Stewart, as the Band of Turnberry showed, leaned towards Bruce. Nor was experience neglected. The bishops were well versed, by the nature of their profession, in administration, as was the Stewart. The Comyns for their part were not inferior in this regard: they had served in the minority of Alexander III. If Duncan of Fife was but a stripling by comparison, he was the senior earl of Scotland and therefore, for that if no other reason, not to be despised. The six carried on the government of Scotland for three hazardous years;[17] their success in that period tells us as much of their ability and their dedication to the task given them in 1286 as of the wisdom of them who chose them. It also tells us much of the true greatness of William Wallace that, in circumstances at least as difficult for Scotland, he was able to assume the office of Guardian with such unchallenged authority. If the choice of the six in 1286 reflects the need for a corporate management, that of William twelve years later indicates how far the situation had changed and the stature of the unique individual who, alone, was judged fit for the office.

At this remove it is tempting to see the ultimate frustration of the work of the 'Guardians of the peace' as inevitable; peace, that is, was impossible to keep. There was, after all, a villain to hand, ready in the wings, awaiting the opportunity to intervene. There was a kingdom beset by problems, lacking the guiding hand of a mature ruler, with a native aristocracy willing to betray the country for their own ends. There was a potential for civil disturbance, fostered by events or interested parties. But if all that appears to constitute a recipe for disaster, that disaster – war with England – did not come until a decade after the death of Alexander III. And when war with England came, Scotland was united against Edward I, however fragile that unity was to be. If Edward I had, as Scottish tradition certainly tells it, been intent from the beginning on bringing Scotland under his control, he was restrained by a subtle patience and the demands of his involvement in Continental affairs from acting at once. If he was relying on the Scottish capacity for self-destruction to ease the accomplishment of a plan for the seizure of Scotland, he was disappointed, for it took the war itself to cause that self-destruction to assume the necessary and desired proportions. The Scots were not yet ready at the death of Alexander III to hand their country over to war and to Edward I. Thus when at Scone in April 1286 they gathered in parliament, they decided to send a delegation to Gascony to seek out Edward, the intention being to inform him of the dispositions made for the government of Scotland in the absence of Margaret of Norway and to ask for his approval. It was not the intention of the Scots to invite his intervention in the affairs of their country. Nor when the delegation, composed of Sir Geoffrey de Mowbray, the Bishop of Brechin, and the Abbot of Jedburgh, finally came upon the English king at the town of Saintes in the modern department of Charente, in September, did he attempt to suggest any such intervention. He allowed the delegation to return to Scotland happy in the optimistic belief that he was sympathetic to the work of the Guardians and the continued independence of Scotland.

When exactly Edward I determined upon the subjugation to his will of the Scots is a matter for speculation. While Alexander III lived, Edward appeared content with the vague definition of the relationship between the two kingdoms which had obtained for so long. The death of Alexander, as we have seen, did not result in immediate action on the part of the English king. How long he would have waited before taking some form of initiative, political or military, it is impossible to say. With his commitments in Wales and France, he needed to be certain that his northern frontier was secure. Alexander's death and the minority of Margaret of Norway threatened that security. Even then Edward, who came back to England from France in the late summer of 1289, made no hostile move against Scotland. His proposal of a marriage between his son, Edward of Carnarvon, and Margaret of Norway was, if not disinterested, statesmanlike;[18] it would have postponed, if it could not prevent, the collision with the Scots. The Guardians for their part saw the virtue in the proposed union, which was agreed in the Treaty of Birgham in 1290, although they were wary enough to sense a possible trap.[19] Edward, his patience, which Wallace was so sorely to test, still intact, confirmed the treaty at Northampton on 28 August. If he accepted that Scotland was to remain free and independent,[20] he had not failed, with his usual attention to detail, to restate in the course of the negotiations his view of his own role in the affairs of the northern kingdom.

At least one writer traces the increased likelihood of war between England and Scotland to the aftermath of the Treaty of Birgham.[21] It was, in his opinion, 'from that point onwards that the pressure was on the Scots, gentle at first but persistent'. It is natural if fruitless to offer a date as a suitable starting-point for the decline into war. This is especially understandable if based on the theory that Edward was himself planning to subjugate Scotland, by force if necessary, as early as Birgham. We may be nearer the truth if we consider the part played in that decline into war by unforeseen circumstances. The death of Alexander III, more importantly perhaps, that of Margaret of Norway in September 1290, were events over which neither Edward nor the Guardians had any control. Each offered Edward an excuse for military intervention; he took neither. But each event made the involvement of Edward in Scotland likelier;[22] the Scots themselves would be forced to call upon him if the alternative was civil war. Once invited, Edward would know well how to profit from a situation which he welcomed, even if he had not himself created it. To say that is not to exonerate him from responsibility or blame for the tragedy of the war which began in 1296. He lived long enough to see the failure of the policy over which he had laboured before 1296 and, perhaps, to understand that he would leave behind him a legacy of bitterness and hatred greater than any which had previously affected relations between the two kingdoms.

The story of how Edward profited from the situation in Scotland and of the events leading to the outbreak of war has been told so often and at such length[23] as to make it unnecessary to repeat it here in any great detail. We need therefore to look at some of the more crucial events as a means of setting the background to the appearance of William Wallace. What he himself made of these events, if indeed he knew anything of them, it is impossible to say. We know only that from the time of his first fame he was, as he remained, Balliol's man.

The death of Margaret of Norway was known in Scotland in early October 1290. As he had in 1286, Robert Bruce, lord of Annandale, despite his advanced age – he was now eighty – moved quickly to protect his interests and to lay claim to the vacant throne. The strongest opposition to that claim lay in the person of John Balliol, lord of Galloway; he had the advantage of the friendship of the Bishop of Durham, Antony Bek, the bellicose friend of Edward I. There were other claimants to the throne; they were not deterred by the weakness of their position. Civil war was closer than it had been in 1286. It did not come. The same commonsense which had prevailed after the death of Alexander III worked again. All those involved in the events of 1290 reached the same conclusion: that recourse should be had to the wisdom of Edward I. If therefore Bishop Fraser of St. Andrews in asking for Edward's intervention pressed the case of John Balliol, others, among them the earls of Angus, Atholl, and Mar, sought that intervention while arguing for Robert Bruce. Edward, recently bereaved by the loss of his beloved wife Eleanor, did not neglect the opportunity. If one Scottish account is to be believed,[24] he was no longer disguising, at least from those about him, his warlike intentions. Words were still to be employed, for Edward loved their use in the cause of his own interests, but he now intended a show of force. From Norham on Tweed where he had taken up residence in the palace of the bishop of Durham, he invited the Scots to meet with him on 30 May 1291. His army he summoned for 3 June. When the Scots appeared before him, he was careful to treat them with respect but struck at once. He would judge the various claims to the throne of Scotland but only upon the acceptance of his paramountcy.[25] Not unnaturally disturbed by this attitude, the Scots were in time forced to agree to Edward's terms.

What Edward's motives were at this time we cannot tell. He had the opportunity to make himself master of Scotland in 1291. The Scots were divided, as they would be again, their morale damaged, their ability to raise an effective opposition gone. It is difficult to see how he could have been prevented from taking over the government of the country. Yet he preferred to enter into a prolonged and unnecessary selection process. If it could be argued that at the end of that process he had, through his choice of John Balliol, in any case made himself master of Scotland, we must still question his wisdom. Edward was renowned through Europe for mental powers, his experience and skill in diplomacy, his Solomon-like qualities.[26] The time for him to seize control of Scotland was in 1291. As he was to learn, even if he was not already conscious of the fact, some of the claimants to the throne of Scotland would be prepared to subordinate the independence of the country to their own interests. He could, had he wished, have used that attitude to ensure his own hold on Scotland; he could, that is, have bought off a number, if not all, of the claimants with land. They were realistic enough to settle for something rather than nothing. It is hard to believe that, of the claimants, only John Hastings was ready to countenance partition if his own case failed. But Edward ignored the opportunity which such thinking presented to him. By doing so, by opting instead for what has been called the 'splendid facade'[27] of sitting in judgement on the claimants to the throne of Scotland, he showed, as he would do later, an inexplicable ineptitude. Ironically, it may be that Edward's failure to act in character in 1291 caused war. He gave the disparate elements in Scotland the time to return to something of the unity of 1286 and by his actions once he had appointed a king guaranteed that that unity would not break in the face of war.

On 17 November 1292, at Berwick, Edward's decision was read by his justice, Roger le Brabazon. Edward had found the case for John Balliol proven. Once enthroned at Scone on St. Andrew's Day, Balliol discovered what kingship meant. Later generations have tended to judge Balliol unsympathetically. We may wonder whether in the circumstances any other claimant would have been more worthy of our sympathy. There was no Scot strong enough to resist Edward. Balliol's opponent, Robert Bruce, known with reason as 'the Competitor', died in the year before the outbreak of war. The man who as long before as 1238, in the reign of Alexander II, had first been seen as heir to the throne, may well have died with a bitter smile on his lips at the thought of Balliol acting at the dictate of Edward I. Bruce's son was ineffectual, his grandson an unknown factor. The time of William Wallace had not yet come. Balliol soon had cause to regret his elevation. If it was natural that Edward should require him, on 26 December, to repeat the oath of homage he had already given in the previous month, Balliol might more readily question the first of the humiliations to which Edward subjected him. A week after Balliol's enthronement, Roger Bartholomew, a burgess of Berwick, appealed to Edward against judgements entered against him in Scottish courts. Edward reversed one judgement. The reversal brought home to the Scots the fact that any promises made by Edward concerning the independence of Scotland were of doubtful value.

The inevitable reaction of the Scots to the reversal was dismissed by Edward. The English king aggravated the situation when in the summer of 1293 his council insisted that the king of Scotland should appear personally to answer any appeals against judgements given in his courts. This was clearly insulting. If Balliol continued for some time to conduct himself with dignity and authority in the face of Edward's pressure, he could not do so indefinitely. If a later account is to be believed, he was in any case disillusioned with his role as king and suspicious of his subjects. On 1 April 1298, his kingdom long lost and himself in custody although not uncomfortable in the London palace of his friend, Antony Bek, Balliol is reported to have said: 'When he possessed and ruled the realm of Scotland as king and lord of the realm, he found in the men of that realm such malice, deceit, treason, and treachery, arising from their malignity, wickedness, and stratagems, and various other execrable and detestable actions'.[28] Having thus attacked the Scots for certain characteristics – from not all of which he himself was free – Balliol went on to maintain that he had feared for an attempt by poison upon his life while he was still king. It is of course possible that Balliol, for good reasons, was saying what he thought his hosts would wish to hear. Moreover, it is unfortunate that at the time of his remarks, his former subjects were, under William Wallace, preparing to face the army of Edward I and that many of them were, within three months, to perish in the defence of his right to the throne of Scotland. Nevertheless, he had been subject to pressure, perhaps verging on the violent, from his own people before the outbreak of war. His own increasing diffidence, not to say fear, when Edward grew more demanding, cannot have endeared him to those who remembered the strength of Scotland when put to the test in 1286.

If there was not in Scotland in early 1294 a war party as such, there was unquestionably a party ready to fight in the event of Edward's exceeding what was considered reasonable. He had come close to that. Clashing with Philip IV of France over Gascony, he now took the step which gave the Scots no further excuse to deceive themselves. Edward called upon his army for France to gather at Portsmouth. His absence from England might have given the Scots, as it gave the Welsh, the opportunity they needed. But they did not even have to wait for him to sail for France. Haughtily and mistakenly, Edward summoned Balliol and various of his subjects, among them William Wallace's feudal superior, James the Stewart, and Bruce the Competitor, then eighty-four years of age, to serve with him in France. Edward had turned the screw too far. The last Scottish king to serve abroad in the army of an English king had been Malcolm IV in 1159. Like Edward with Balliol, Henry II had established a sort of mental superiority over Malcolm.[29] But not even Balliol dared to go as far with Edward as Malcolm had gone with Henry, neither he nor the others summoned by Edward complied.

War with England could not now be prevented. The Scots began to seek allies and, understandably, turned to France. Philip IV was agreeable to discussions. In July 1295 four representatives were named to negotiate a treaty with the French king. They were William Fraser, Matthew of Crambeth, John de Soules, and the quaintly named and intriguing Ingram de Umfraville. They travelled to France and on 23 October concluded an offensive and defensive alliance with Philip.[30] The treaty was ratified in Scotland on 23 February 1296. What Balliol himself thought of these events is not recorded. Whether he wished it or not, he was at the head of a people ready for war. He was truly, as one chronicler aptly put it, 'a lamb among wolves'.[31]

Edward, meanwhile, had been diverted by the rebellion in Wales. He postponed sailing to France and dealt with it. That done, he had decided that he could no longer defer action against Scotland. France would have to wait. It is impossible not to admire the energy with which the king, fifty-eight years old, faced with problems in France, wearied after the Welsh campaign, embittered by what he believed to be the treason of the Scots, flung himself against them. He ordered his army to assemble before him at Newcastle upon Tyne on 1 March 1296, arranged for a fleet of ships to sail from East Anglia round the coast to provision the army, and set out to punish those who had defied him. Those who were the target of his wrath had themselves issued their own call to arms to their fellow-countrymen. In the name of John Balliol, the Scottish feudal host was summoned to meet on 11 March four miles north of Selkirk, at Caddonlee. Not all the principal Scots chose to obey the summons. Not least among these were the earls of Dunbar and Angus. But more striking and disturbing was the attitude adopted by the Bruces. They stood apart. It may be true that their behaviour was 'clear and consistent', as one biographer of Robert I has put it.[32] They owed no loyalty to Balliol. They held to their oath given in 1292 to Edward. He had flattered their hope of, one day, replacing Balliol.[33] A precedent had been set. If William Wallace had known the reasoning of the Bruces, he would have despised it. Wherever he was, he was unlikely to have disregarded the summons to Caddonlee.

The war which followed was characterised in its early stages in two particular ways. First, it was an exceptionally brutal war, on both sides. On Easter Monday a Scottish army, under seven earls, crossed the Solway. The size of the army is unknown, but we can be in no doubt about their intentions. In the words of the Lanercost Chronicle the Scots began 'burning houses, slaughtering men and driving off cattle, and on the two following days they violently assaulted the city of Carlisle; but failing in their attempt, they retired on the third day'.[34] This is a sober and restrained account of what must have been horrifying. It was a rehearsal for worse still. In April the Scots raided into Northumberland. Again they burned houses, but now added sacrilege to their crimes. They burned churches and monasteries, and are reported to have burned alive a group of schoolboys, perhaps as many as two hundred, at Corbridge.[35] What the purpose of these raids was we can only guess. They were futile, failed to break Edward's resolve, wasted energy, and diverted attention from what must be the main issue, the defeat of Edward.

He had not been idle. His response to the raid of the seven earls was the sack of Berwick. This was far in excess of anything the Scots had perpetrated and must cast doubt, again, on his stability. Whereas, at the time of the execution of Wallace, he had had nine years of frustrations and disappointments, he had no such excuse at Berwick. The failure of his first attack on the town, the jeers of the defenders, his own impatience and sense of betrayal, do not explain the slaughter which he condoned and even encouraged once the walls of the town were breached. For two days he allowed his army to kill and burn. Berwick, despite his own later efforts to rebuild and restore it, was never again to achieve its former status. If, strictly speaking, he had adhered to the rules of war in handing over to sack a town which had refused to surrender, Berwick was the first, and perhaps along with the execution of Wallace, the greatest stain on his reputation.

The second feature of the war at this time was the military ineptitude of the Scottish leaders. We have seen the futility of their raids into England. They were no more successful when put to a test for which, in theory at least, they ought to have been better prepared. From Berwick Edward moved slowly, confidently, north in the direction of Dunbar. He may have felt that Berwick was the true measure of the Scots' competence. Success may have bred a certain complacency. If this was the case, it was imperative that the Scots strike back effectively, in order to redress the balance. Although the earl of Dunbar, Patrick, was Edward's man, his castle had fallen into the hands of the Scots through the stratagem of his wife, who had embraced the Scottish cause.[36] Edward detached a cavalry force under John de Warenne, earl of Surrey, to recapture Dunbar. The Scots now scorned the opportunity for the ambush of Warenne or for any tactic other than the obvious one. There was no reason why they should meet Surrey in the open field, and pit cavalry against cavalry. Where the English, the Welsh campaigns behind them, were experienced and hardened, the Scots were untried. This did not deter them. With a sublime arrogance, they accepted what they took to be a challenge. There was no Wallace among them to dissuade them, to put the alternatives before them. They could have delayed any form of action at this time, for Dunbar was not worth the risk of defeat. They could have drawn the English on, as Wallace did before Falkirk – a tactic adopted by Robert I. They could have allowed the lengthening of the English lines of communication to work against the invaders.

That they did none of these things doomed them. Even then, patience and discipline in the ranks of the cavalry might still have won the day. Surrey, as Wallace would clearly demonstrate at Stirling, was not an exceptional soldier, but he knew enough to profit from the Scottish abandonment of a good position. Warenne had divided his force; one section he left before Dunbar to contain the garrison, the other he led to face the Scottish army. That army, sensing an opening which did not in reality exist, broke ranks and rushed to the attack. No doubt it was a splendid sight. No doubt it was exhilarating. But it ended in disaster. From the safety of a hill, the Scots had charged into defeat. Surrey's troops had no difficulty in dealing with the Scots whose own impetuosity had made the outcome certain. As quickly as they had attacked the Scots turned, intent on reaching Selkirk Forest, where not many months later a wiser man laid his own, different plans.

Surrey's victory at Dunbar effectively ended resistance to Edward. It was scarcely a battle; it is difficult to think of it even as an engagement but rather as a rout. How many fought at Dunbar, how many were killed, we have no means of knowing. An English version which numbers the Scottish dead at over ten thousand is hardly credible.[37] The foot soldiers, left to their own devices by their leaders, suffered heavily. Many Scots of high position fell into English hands and were distributed in various prisons.[38] Of those who joined Sir William Douglas, Wallace's future ally, taken at Berwick, among the prisoners was the young Andrew Murray, also to be associated with Wallace. They learned enough from the disaster at Berwick and the farce at Dunbar to recognise the need for change. It was unfortunate that those who did learn were to continue in the minority for some time.

After Dunbar, Edward undertook a leisurely progress through what was, in essence, his kingdom of Scotland. To emphasise his authority he caused the symbolic Stone of Destiny to be carried from Scone to Westminster Abbey. One after another the castles of Scotland were turned over to him. Balliol, meanwhile, bereft of ideas, slipped away before him. At length he begged for terms. He was forced to agree to a succession of public appearances in which he confessed to a variety of offences against Edward and, in the last act, he surrendered his kingdom to Edward on 10 July at Brechin. If humiliated, he kept his life, and was sent to the Tower of London, escorted by the earl of Lancaster. He remained a scapegoat for the failure of the nation as a whole and entered the Scottish consciousness as 'Toom Tabard', the pathetic, broken figure of Brechin of whom Wyntoun wrote:

> This Johun the Balliol dispoyilyeide he
> Off al his robis and ryalte.
> The pellour that tuk out of his tabart,
> Tuyme Tabart he was callit efftirwart;
> And all othir insignyis
> That fel to kynge on ony wise,
> Baythe septure, suerde, crowne and rynge,
> Fra this Johun, that he made kynge,
> Hallely fra hym he tuk thar,
> And mad hym of his kynrik bare.[39]

Edward returned to Berwick in late August. There he produced his plan for the government of Scotland. He entrusted the functioning of it to

Surrey, who was to be lieutenant or keeper. To assist Surrey, Edward named as treasurer Hugh Cressingham and as chancellor Walter of Amersham. His chief justice in the newly conquered kingdom was to be William Ormsby.[40] He placed his officials in other lesser posts, assured himself of the safety of the castles, and in all things was, as always, thorough. He had reason to be pleased with himself. There remained one other task before he left Scotland to the care of his subordinates. All substantial landholders were required to give, or renew, their oath of loyalty to Edward as lord of Scotland. Whatever the actual number of those who swore fealty to Edward at Berwick,[41] the name of William Wallace is not to be found among them. It may well be, as Barrow argues,[42] more surprising that the name of his older brother, Malcolm, who had inherited Elderslie, is absent. But nothing can alter the symbolic importance since attached to the absence from the 'Ragman Roll' of the name of William Wallace.[43]

NOTES

1. For genealogical tables relating to Alexander III and the subsequent disputed succession see, for example, Dickinson, *op. cit.*, 53 & 151; Barrow: *Robert Bruce*, 455; McNair Scott, xiv.

2. Barrow: *Robert Bruce*, 9.

3. Lanercost, 40, tells of Alexander's addiction to the pleasures of the flesh during his widowhood.

4. As an introduction to Alexander's reign see Dickinson, *passim*; Powicke: *The Thirteenth Century*, 1953, 589-598.

5. A recent study of the Treaty of Perth is to be found in Lustig: 'The Treaty of Perth, a re-examination', *S.H.R.*, LVIII, April 1979, 35-57.

6 Dickinson, chap. 8; Barrow: *Kingdom*, chap. 4; Powicke, 574 & 588-9.

7. Barrow: *Robert Bruce*, 13-15.

8. Dickinson, 110.

9. Wyntoun, 266.

10. *Foedera*, 1, ii, 638.

11. Palgrave, *Documents and Records*, 42.

12. The most recent treatment of the Guardians is Reid: 'The Kingless Kingdom: The Scottish Guardianships of 1286-1306', *S.H.R.*, vol. LXI, Oct. 1982, 105-129.

13. Lanercost, 117.

14. Palgrave, *Documents and Records*, 42.

15. On this question see, for example, Barron, 112 and Dickinson, 144, both of whom find in the agreement a statement of support for Robert Bruce the Competitor's claim to the throne, while Powicke, 598n and Barrow: *Robert Bruce*, 26, offer another opinion.

16. The presence of James the Stewart at Turnberry prompts the tentative suggestion that the troubles in the south-west were the sort of adventure which might appeal to a

younger, landless son. For Wallace to have participated it would, of course, be necessary to accept that the date of his birth was earlier than is usually adopted.

17. According to Lanercost, 59, he was inferior to none in the baseness of his character. He is described as being 'cruel and greedy beyond average'.

18. In 1289 Alexander Comyn earl of Buchan died from natural causes at an advanced age; Duncan of Fife, perhaps not surprisingly, if Lanercost is accurate in its assessment of his personality, was murdered by his own kinsmen.

19. Ferguson: *Scotland's Relations with England,* 1977, 22-24; Barrow: *Robert Bruce,* 40ff.

20. Ferguson, 23.

21. Barrow: *Robert Bruce,* 40-41.

22. Ferguson, 23.

23. Barrow: *Robert Bruce,* 41-2.

24. Most notably in Barrow: *Robert Bruce,* chaps. 1-4. Shorter accounts can be found in Barron, chap. 1; Dickinson, chap. 16: Powicke, 598–607; Prestwich: *The Three Edwards: War and State in England 1272-1377,* 1980, chap. 2.

25. Fordun, 308.

26. Rishanger, 241.

27. He had been asked to use his good offices in the war between Castile and France in the early years of his reign. See Salzman: *Edward I,* 1968, 49-50.

28. Ferguson, 24; *McNair Scott,* 27.

29. Stones (ed.): *Anglo-Scottish relations 1174-1328,* 1964, no. 27.

30. Warren: *Henry II,* 1983, 69, 182, and *passim.*

31. Barrow: *Robert Bruce,* 90-91.

32. Rishanger, 371.

33. McNair Scott, 34.

34. He showed himself in his true colours in his famous retort to the Competitor's son when the latter reminded him of his promise: 'Have we nothing else to do but win kingdoms for you?' *Chron. Bower,* ii. 166.

35. Lanercost, 115.

36. Palgrave, *Documents and Records,* 149.

37. Guisborough, 277-8.

38. Cotton, 312.

39. Stevenson, ii. 26; *Cal. Docs. Scot.* ii, 742.

40. Wyntoun, 295.

41. Barrow: *Robert Bruce,* 106-7 has brief details of Edward's appointments.

42. Barrow: *Robert Bruce,* 107-9 argues that the number actually present at Berwick could not have reached the figure of two thousand and thus contradicts the view so often held.

43. Barrow, *Robert Bruce,* 109.

CHAPTER 3

The Time of Victory, 1297

Edward left Scotland on 17 September 1296. If preoccupied with affairs across the Channel, he had reason to feel satisfied with the campaign he had just completed. The opposition, where it had not faded before him, had been futile, ill-conceived and badly led. Balliol had been ridiculed and exiled; no natural successor was available, even if Edward had been prepared to entertain the idea of a second puppet king. The war party in Scotland had been broken and many of its members were in English prisons. It is hardly surprising if Edward gave no apparent thought to a further rebellion against his authority. He knew of no source for rebellion; that there could be any potential leaders of opposition to be found outside the ranks of those he had so easily defeated never occurred to him. His blindness to the alternatives was shared by the Scots nobility. They like Edward had been raised to think of themselves as unique; failure, like success, opened no new avenues for them.

Something of Edward's contempt for Scotland and the Scots may be gleaned from a remark attributed to him at the time of his departure from Scotland.[1] It was directed to Surrey. As one old soldier to another, Edward is reported to have said: 'Bon besoiogne fait qy de merde se delivrer'. He had been less coarse but equally dismissive when the son of the Competitor, Robert lord of Annandale, reminded him, no doubt timidly, of the promise of the throne of Scotland. Edward, with Balliol defeated, no longer needed to placate the likes of Bruce for whom he had the same contempt he had for other Scots. 'Have we nothing to do but win kingdoms for you?' he snarled at the unfortunate Bruce. Edward never lost that attitude to the Scots, although he was not always so forthright; to achieve his ends he would use whatever approach he thought appropriate.

His crossing of the Tweed back into England was not the signal for an immediate rising against the government for which he had made Surrey responsible. The nature of Edward's hold, in military and political terms, over the Scots ensured that for some months at least there would be a lull. Neither Surrey nor Cressingham, any more than Edward himself, can fairly be blamed for failing to realise that it would be no more than a lull. If Surrey and Cressingham can be charged with arrogance,[2] they had cause.

They had seen and been a party to their king's achievements in Scotland. Surrey himself had, with little effort and few losses, chased from the field the best of the Scots. Only time would show how transient Edward's first success in Scotland was. The situation in the autumn of 1296 was in line with the pattern of Edward's relationship with Scotland for the rest of his life. If he himself was in the field or held the reins of government close, his supremacy was safe, certainly in military terms. It was as if he exercised some sort of mental hold upon the Scots, Wallace apart. His reputation, or their perception of it, appeared to negate the drive of the Scots. Against his ruthless practicality, their actions are seen as mere posturings. His preparations for a campaign were more thorough,[3] his assessment of the factors involved more realistic, his judgement of the commitment of the Scots more experienced. It may well be true that, in Barron's words, 'after Stirling Bridge the Scots under Wallace never won a victory in the open against any English force which could fairly be described as an army'.[4] Barron, of course, is pursuing in this context a comparison of his hero, Andrew Murray, with William Wallace, to the latter's detriment. Barron's passionate championship of Murray is a useful and important corrective to the lack of balance existing before. He does not, however, deal with one significant question: which of the Scots, while Edward was in charge of the English forces, achieved what he accuses Wallace of failing to do? Murray himself died before he could face the ultimate test of a Scottish commander: an engagement with an English army led by Edward in person.[5] Stirling, the credit for which Murray shares, was, in any case, a pitched battle: are we to assume that the decision to fight was Wallace's alone, that Murray allowed himself to be persuaded against his better judgement to fight? If that is so, it speaks badly for the powers of leadership which Barron so eloquently defends. When we turn from Andrew Murray to Robert I, we find that his victory at Loudoun Hill on or about 10 May 1307 may seem, at first sight, to contradict the argument of Edward's infallibility against the Scots. Bruce, however, never fought against Edward. At Loudoun Hill, he was opposed by Edward's lieutenant in Scotland, Aymer de Valence, earl of Pembroke, who had sent him scurrying away from Methven in the previous June.[6] Bruce at this period was an opportunist and a quick learner, creditable qualities in a general, no doubt, but perhaps not sufficient to bring victory against Edward I in his prime. When Edward left Scotland in September 1296, he was, as far as the Scots were concerned, in his prime, his superiority over them as yet unquestioned.

It was a superiority which, being personal, was not long to survive his departure. The great king, for once, had not shown his customary skill in the selection of subordinates to govern Scotland in his absence. Surrey, some few years older than Edward, was not enthusiastic about exercising in person the authority he had been given. The victor of Dunbar preferred to take his ease on his estates in Yorkshire; he feared for his health, we are told, in the unpleasant air of Scotland.[7] Cressingham, the treasurer, saw the chance to better himself while Surrey remained in Yorkshire. Of illegitimate birth and somewhat unprepossessing,[8] Cressingham, seconded by his colleague, William Ormsby, the justiciar, effectively ran the government. He was soon unpopular with the Scots both in himself and in his official capacity.[9] By May of 1297 Cressingham was facing a series of insurrections throughout the country. Despite Stirling, Cressingham was neither a fool nor lacking in something of the energy which characterised his master. He was rather the victim of a force which could not be withstood.

Cressingham was given little time before that force was loosed upon him. Traditionally but inaccurately, the signal for rebellion was the murder by Wallace of the English sheriff of Lanark some time in May 1297. That date reflects the dominance of Wallace but we know that there were disturbances over a wide area – whether spontaneous or organised is unclear – well before then. It is unlikely that all who participated in these disturbances were inspired by the highest motives. The activities of Edward's officials must have been a factor; not all would be indifferent to abusing their position. There was, inevitably, discontent with Cressingham's enthusiastic levying of taxes in the name of his king. It can be assumed, equally, that English justice, as administered by Ormsby, would meet with resistance. Some of those who took to arms must have hoped, for their own ends, to benefit from the lack of English garrisons in the more isolated areas. Itinerant outlaw bands would be attracted by news of what would soon threaten to lead to anarchy. A minor success against the occupying forces would breed confidence. If there were thus squalid motives for involvement in the struggle, many who participated were, beyond dispute, genuinely patriotic, determined upon ridding the land of a detested enemy, upon disproving the myth of English invincibility.

The effect of the disturbances which appear to have begun in the early months of 1297 was, whatever lay behind them, considerable. In the western highlands, in Aberdeenshire, down in the south-west in Galloway, there were reports of violence and upheaval.[10] No one, let alone Cressingham, could have co-ordinated action against the insurgents over such an area. Had action been possible, the weather, like the distances involved, would have militated against the necessary response. The time was well chosen, the tactics of the insurgents realistic; a lesson had been learned from the campaign of 1296. What prompted the timing and the change in approach we do not know. If there was a single guiding hand behind the disturbances, it was surely that of a genius.

That there was subsequently such a guiding hand became the firm opinion of the English. It is interesting that the names advanced were not those of the two men most closely identified in the popular imagination with the destruction of English power in 1297, William Wallace and Andrew Murray. Rather, the English saw in Robert Wishart, bishop of Glasgow, and James the Stewart the instigators of rebellion. This belief was not without foundation. If Edward attempted to appoint English rather than Scottish priests to Scottish benefices, he was bound to arouse resentment. The Church in Scotland already possessed the framework for the dissemination of rebellious ideas and the integration of one uprising with another. To the English, therefore, it was peopled with subversives. The Chronicle of Lanercost was emphatic on this point: 'In like manner, as we know that it is truly written, that evil priests are the cause of the people's ruin, so the ruin of the realm of Scotland had its source within the bosom of her own Church; because whereas they who ought to have led them, misled them, they became a snare and a stumbling block of iniquity towards them, and brought them all to ruin. For with one accord both those who discharged the office of prelate and those who were preachers, corrupted the ears and minds of nobles and commons, by advice and exhortation, both publicly and secretly, stirring them to enmity against that king and nation who had so effectively delivered them; declaring falsely that it was far more justifiable to attack them than the Saracens'.[11]

Wishart, who lived until 1316 and thus saw the triumph of Robert I, was without doubt a persistent supporter of the Scottish cause and therefore deserved the abuse of the English.[12] As for the noble James the Stewart, he belonged to that category about which another English chronicler was no less scathing than Lanercost, if somewhat more restrained in his language. It was Cressingham's opinion that the Scottish lords were not to be trusted in this year of 1297, and Walter of Hemingburgh shares the treasurer's suspicions. He tells us that wherever their bodies might be, 'even when . . . present with the king . . . at heart they were on the opposite side'.[13] It is, however, when we turn again to Lanercost that we find the bishop and the Stewart linked in what is seen as a common culpability: 'Hardly had a period of six months passed since the Scots had bound themselves by the above-mentioned solemn oath of fidelity and subjection to the King of the English, when the reviving malice of that perfidious race excited their minds to fresh sedition. For the bishop of the Church in

Glasgow, whose personal name was Robert Wishart, ever foremost in treason, conspired with the Steward of the realm named James, for a new piece of insolence, yea, for a new chapter of ruin. Not daring openly to break their pledged faith to the king, they caused a certain bloody man, William Wallace, who had been chief of brigands in Scotland, to revolt against the king and assemble the people in his support'.[14]

Here we have Wishart and the Stewart not merely guilty of breaking their oath to Edward and indulging in a conspiracy against him but in league with the most notorious outlaw and rebel of them all. Just as we cannot place Wallace's first action against the English with any certainty before May 1297, so we are ignorant of the role of Wishart and the Stewart in events before then. It is reasonable to suppose that, perhaps like Wallace, they profited from a situation not of their making. If that is the case, we are left with the fact that the earlier disturbances were spontaneous and haphazard, not the work of any one person or group. This does not reduce the value to the Scottish cause of Wishart and the Stewart any more than it lessens the impact of Wallace.

What is to be made of Lanercost's statement that Wishart and the Stewart persuaded Wallace to rebel? Failing reliable evidence to the contrary, we are free to believe that Wallace was a faithful son of the Church in Scotland. His later violence against English priests suggests an almost pathological hatred of those who had, as he understood it, persecuted the Scottish Church.[15] It is a big step from accepting that loyalty to the Church, from accepting also that Wallace was an ally of Wishart and the Stewart in 1297, sharing their views, to agreeing that they had led him into rebellion against Edward I. However little we know of Wallace, it can be said with some assurance that he was, if nothing else, his own man. He can be pictured listening to the other two, giving them the respect due to them by reason of their station, sympathising with their distress at the English occupation of Scotland. Perhaps they were better able to articulate the emotions which all felt. It is far less easy to visualise him being led by these two representatives of that class which had so dismally failed to uphold the honour and freedom of Scotland in 1296. It is quite conceivable that as a preliminary he asked Wishart's blessing – no doubt speedily given – for the undertaking upon which he was entering. Nor can it be denied that his feudal relationship with the Stewart was of value to him;[16] from James he would be happy to receive the pledge of support. All of this would be in keeping with his dedication to due form which manifested itself in its most extreme, and fatal, form in his allegiance to Balliol.

Such formalities apart, Wallace required no prodding, no permission. He was, then as always, fully capable of making up his own mind. We have only to compare the fierce, even explosive, nature of his conduct in May 1297 with the dithering of Wishart and the Stewart in June and July to see the truth.[17] The English determination to denigrate Wallace at all costs may help us to understand why he is portrayed as subordinate to Wishart and the Stewart. Only by relegating him to a supporting role – all that his social origins entitled him to – could his achievement be explained. Those who wrote of him in this way could not see that, with Wallace, a new age was beginning. He rose to prominence through his own ability. What is true of Wallace – that he was essentially his own inspiration – was true of the friend and colleague he was about to make, Andrew Murray.[18]

The threads of the resistance to Edward I came together in the persons of Andrew Murray and William Wallace in the late summer of 1297. It is appropriate to rank Murray first for the reason that we know more of him at this time than we do of Wallace. The son of Sir Andrew Murray of Petty, he was present at the débâcle of Dunbar and there, with his father and uncle, made prisoners.[19] During his incarceration at Chester he had occasion to reflect upon the futility of the Scottish tactics at Dunbar. Escaping from Chester,[20] he made his way to the family lands in Moray and there, secure from English interference, planned rebellion. It does no disservice to Murray, 'one of the chivalric figures of Scottish history' as he has been called,[21] to stress that, unlike Wallace, his prominence in the early days of his fame depended upon his position in society. He had, after all, gained no reputation as a soldier; Dunbar was no recommendation. That shadowy and intriguing figure, Alexander Pilche, burgess of Inverness,[22] may well have been a more potent factor in the north than Murray. But there is no question that, once he chose to exercise it, leadership of this part of the rebellion lay with Murray as of right. With Pilche and those others who had already made their mark on events added to his own following, Murray had a formidable force at his disposal. Mobile, urgent, impassioned, they struck at the English with such effect as can best be measured from the pleas for help sent from the north to Edward.[23] If the writers of these pleas, 'diligent and faithful friends' of the English king as they were careful to describe themselves, were prone to hide behind the excuse of superior enemy numbers – Murray, they said, led 'a very large body of rogues'[24] – we cannot doubt that the pressure upon them was intense. It must be a matter of regret that we do not know the source of the new Scottish tactics, for such they were. It is quite understandable that the likes of Pilche should rely upon hit and run. But what of Murray himself? He had been raised in a tradition which, as Dunbar demonstrated, was both outmoded and self-destructive. Yet it does appear that, once returned to his homeland from Chester, he had no difficulty in adapting to the situation. Did he come to realise, once involved, that the tactics of Pilche and the others with him were the only ones suitable in the circumstances? Or had he reached the obvious conclusion while a prisoner of the English? If we had the answer to this problem we might be closer to a realistic assessment of the respective merits of Murray and Wallace. All that can be said with any pretensions to accuracy is that Murray was swift to learn and a charismatic leader of the rebellion in the north. Throughout the summer, from May to August, he continued to pose an insuperable problem for the English and their supporters. Arrogantly he laid siege to Castle Urquhart, and although foiled in that attempt, he was not diverted from his purpose. He took from the English other castles, Inverness, Elgin, and Banff among them.

Edward had not been slow to react to news of the events in the north. Not all Scots were sympathetic to Murray; on them Edward had relied to keep the country quiet. Murray had not taken long to prove that the administration, in which Henry Cheyne, bishop of Aberdeen, and Effie Countess of Ross ranked high, could not cope with him. To stiffen their resolve, Edward released from the retinue of Scottish lords whom he had summoned to join him on his Continental expedition, John of Badenoch and John earl of Buchan, both of them Comyns.[25] They, like a number of other Scottish lords, were perhaps less dedicated to the English cause than Edward would have wished. That at least was the opinion of Cressingham who was driven to report to Edward in the following terms: 'The peace on the other side of the Scottish Sea is still in obscurity, as it is said, as to the doings of the earls who are there. But at all events we hope that if our business succeeds well on the day of Saint Laurence as to the Bishop of Glasgow and the others, as far as the people on the other side of the Scottish Sea are concerned, we hope soon to have them at our pleasure by God's grace. Sir Andrew de Rait[26] is going to you with a credence, which he has shown to me, and which is false in many points and obscure, as will be shown hereafter, as I fear; and, therefore, sire, if it be your pleasure, you will give little weight to it'.[27]

Thus Cressingham relayed both his suspicions and his concern.[28] Indeed, Cressingham had seen his suspicions confirmed. By the time he was writing to Edward,[29] the volatile nature of the Scottish lords had already declared itself.[30] But both they and Cressingham had been overtaken by one far greater than they. In May, William Wallace, in the words of Fordun, had 'raised his head'. It is a curiously effective and telling phrase. Wallace, we learn from it, had suddenly erupted upon the scene, no longer obscure, to embody henceforth the spirit of Scottish nationalism. With the murder of the sheriff of Lanark, he sprang full-blown, as it were, into the national conscience and has remained there since. It was an act which was accorded a significance which it has not lost.

As is so often the case with Wallace, the events of May 1297 are unclear. The reason for the murder of William Heselrig, Edward's sheriff of Lanark, escapes us even now. The traditional account has not lost its potency. As recently as 1982, a biographer of Robert I repeats it:[31]

'Wallace had become a magnet for the discontented. He had recently married a young woman who lived in Lanark. Visiting her by stealth, as a marked man, he clashed with an English patrol. Fighting his way clear, he retreated to her house and as his pursuers hammered on the front door he escaped by the back to the rocky Cartland Crags. Enraged by the failure to capture him, Sir William Heselrig,[32] Sheriff of Lanark, ordered the house to be burned and all within it, wife and servants, to be put to the sword. From that day Wallace vowed an undying vengeance against the English.

'Gathering together a band of desperate men, he fell by night on the sheriff and his armed guard, hewed the sheriff into small pieces with his own sword and burned the buildings and those within them.

'For the first time one of the high officials of the hated conquerors had been slain and a ripple of jubilation spread through the oppressed'.

What we are offered here is the account by Blind Harry,[33] rendered into today's English. Wallace thus gains his revenge for the murder of his beloved in that bloody fashion which so characterises him in the work of Blind Harry. Heselrig, in this scenario, cannot simply be killed; his body must be dismembered.[34] Those who made up the sheriff's suite, whether they had played a part in the murder of Marion Braidfute or not, cannot escape retribution and must be made to suffer, and with appropriate horror.[35] Measured against certain of Wallace's later recorded actions, this version of events at Lanark, open to question though it may be, has the ring of authenticity. The fate of Heselrig compares with that of Cressingham after Stirling. The burning of buildings in Lanark differs only in scale from what Wallace did in the north of England. The burning alive of English soldiers was something of which he was capable, especially if the story of the Barns of Ayr is based on fact.[36] That Wallace behaved violently at Lanark is indisputable. He was a ferocious man; however motivated, he employed no half-measures when faced with the enemy.

The origins of Wallace's ferociousness at Lanark need not lie in the death of Marion Braidfute. She, like another and far more celebrated Marion in an earlier age, belongs to the outlaw tradition rather than to history. Revenge may, of course, have taken Wallace to Lanark, revenge for an unknown friend or for other actions on the part of the English. A less romantic era, such as our own, might look for the reason for the murder of

Heselrig in more reliable if pedestrian sources. Perhaps the most important clue to the circumstances is to be discovered in the indictment laid against Wallace at his trial in 1305.[37] There he was charged with having slain Heselrig on a day when the latter was holding a county court in Lanark. If this is the case, two explanations may be offered for Wallace's actions. The first is that he had personal reasons for murdering Heselrig. Heselrig in his official capacity may have entered some judgement against Wallace which led to a quarrel, then to murder. It will be remembered that neither Wallace's own name nor that of his brother Malcolm appeared on the Ragman Roll. Should that omission indicate that one or both of the brothers had been outlawed or found guilty of some offence against Edward, Heselrig's assize at Lanark may have been connected to the previous event. Wallace's descent on Lanark may therefore have been prompted by a desire to right a wrong; a refusal or threat on the part of the unfortunate sheriff may have brought about his death. The second explanation, more perhaps in keeping with Wallace's reputation, is that the assize at Lanark offered the chance to strike a blow at the representative of the English king as he was dispensing justice to an oppressed people. Wallace, therefore, would have no personal reason for acting. This second explanation, at least in retrospect, would seem symbolic, as was the absence of the Wallace name from the Ragman Roll.

It is debateable whether Wallace's motives at Lanark mattered at all. Premeditated or not, the timing of the murder was remarkable. Much of Scotland was already in a ferment; news of the disturbances could not entirely be suppressed by the authorities. The murder of Heselrig, dramatic, barbarous, had an immediate impact. Heselrig's death had several consequences. Of these, one perhaps has not always been given sufficient emphasis. Whatever his status before Lanark, Wallace was now an outlaw, one whom Edward was unlikely to pardon.[38] Like Bruce after Dumfries, Wallace after Lanark could not go back to what he had been. He was no longer anonymous; he was now identified as an enemy, soon no doubt to be the prey, of the English king. At Lanark Wallace had posed a challenge and offered an insult; Edward was not the man to ignore either. Strangely, however, in the light of the later significance attached to the murder of Heselrig, we can find no evidence of Edward's own reaction. This contrasts vividly with his behaviour in 1306 when he was informed of the incident at Dumfries. At first apparently loath to believe in Bruce's guilt, he did at length order action of the most extreme kind. Aymer de Valence was instructed, as Barbour tells us, 'to burn and slay and raise dragon',[39] and Edward without doubt planned for Bruce the same punishment he had inflicted on Wallace. If in 1297 he was as angered by the murder of Heselrig, we have no proof of it. His later viciousness is usually explained by the events of the intervening years and his own instability. Despite this, one cannot but wonder why, as far as we are aware, Wallace did not in 1297 seem to affect him personally.

Nonetheless, Wallace in May 1297 may be said to have had no alternative to full-scale rebellion. In this he could not have succeeded, unless he was acknowledged to be of the stuff of heroes. After Lanark he did not run into hiding; he was available, visible, potent. For once English and Scottish chroniclers agree; Wallace's original band of some thirty men grew at once. It is to be expected that in the English accounts those who joined him would be characterised as scum and criminals. Thus we read: 'He [Wallace] . . . convoked all who were outlawed to himself, and acted as if he were the chief of them, and they increased to many people'.[40] Guisborough's description of Wallace's followers, who in his eyes are nothing but 'vagrants, fugitives, and outlaws', is balanced on the Scottish side by Fordun.[41] Here more honourable motives are ascribed to the Scots: 'From that time there were gathered to him all who were of bitter heart and were weighed down beneath the burden of bondage under the intolerable rule of English domination, and he became their leader'. For these unfortunates, rebellion was preferable to slavery. The calibre of person drawn to Wallace, whether we accept the one or the other version of events, cannot have been high. It tells us much of his ability that he was able to weld them into a coherent and successful force; no mere rabble could have defeated the English at Stirling.

In the increase in his force we may find a second consequence of the murder of Heselrig. It has been argued above that the assertion of the Lanercost chronicler that the bishop of Glasgow and James the Stewart inspired Wallace to rebellion is erroneous. His success at Lanark in killing the representative of the English king, and its effect upon recruitment, cannot have been unknown to the other two. It is at this point, rather than earlier, that they are likelier to have become involved with Wallace. Here was the opening for these rather timid men to stand with the new hero, to give him advice, above all perhaps, to provide men, horses, equipment. This is a less important role than Lanercost allocates to them. It is not to be disparaged, however. The support of Wishart and the Stewart, given their standing in Scotland, must have guaranteed Wallace a certain legitimacy and, with it, power.

With Heselrig dead, Wallace acted with great energy. That he was able to move, apparently, with total freedom cannot wholly have been the consequence of Lanark. A riposte on the part of the English was called for; no such is recorded. The English administration was either paralysed by the speed of events both in the west and elsewhere or unable for some reason to put troops in the field. The propaganda value of Lanark was considerable, no doubt, but Wallace was allowed a space in which to plan and carry out his next endeavour. Heselrig had been an important official but Wallace now aimed for a more senior figure. He raced to Scone where William Ormsby, the justiciar, was in residence, like Heselrig the dispenser of Edward's justice. At Wallace's side was a new colleague, Sir William Douglas, who had surrendered the castle of Berwick to Edward in the previous year. It did not require the sack of Berwick, where the inhabitants 'fell like autumn leaves',[42] to turn Douglas to violence. He was already notorious, guilty of the abduction of a rich widow and of murder.[43] With Berwick lost, he had disappeared from the accounts of events. Now he came to the forefront once more, attracted to Wallace by the opportunity for the violence which meant so much to him.

The raid upon Scone, some eighty miles from Lanark, was carried out on horseback. The mounts may have been Douglas's contribution to Wallace's force. Wallace almost succeeded in his intention. Ormsby, however, learned of his approach and fled but, like Edward II after Byland, was forced to leave valuables behind.[44] If Wallace had failed in his primary intention, of ridding Scotland of another English official, the raid encouraged further action against the forces of the occupation. The rebellion flared between the Forth and the Tay, with the support of Macduff, the son of the earl of Fife. The English were forced behind the walls of their castles, against which the Scots could do little, although Wallace himself would later return to besiege Dundee.

At his trial in 1305, Wallace would be charged with atrocities committed during the war. These included the murder of English clerics. This was not a charge he dignified with an answer, perhaps because it was true. If the worst atrocities were committed either at his order or in defiance of him during the raid into England after Stirling, it seems that as early as the summer of 1297, attacks were being made upon English clergy. If we are to believe Guisborough,[45] the Scots, foiled perhaps by the retreat of the English soldiers into their castles, vented their spleen on such unfortunate clergy as they could lay their hands on. Neither age nor sex saved lives: 'They [the Scots] took old men, priests and women of the English nation (whom they had specially kept alive for the purpose) to bridges over the rivers; and when they had tied their hands or feet together so that they could not swim, they threw them or pushed them into the water, laughing and jeering as they struggled and went under'. For sport, others were brought to trial before Wallace himself, 'that bandit' as Guisborough calls him. Still others were seized from sanctuary and butchered.

If Guisborough was not concerned, any more than other chroniclers, with strict accuracy where Wallace was concerned, it is to be expected that the Scots would not distinguish between any of the hated English who fell into their hands. Berwick was too recent a memory and the Scottish clergy themselves were not moved by Christian charity towards their English brethren. A precedent and a tradition had been set from the beginning of the war and Wallace would not restrain his men even if he had wanted to. As he had shown at Lanark, he was fully alive to the use to which atrocity could be put. It had brought him recruits then and stultified the English response; he had no cause to change his approach afterwards.

Whether inspired by the example of Wallace or not, those Scots who had failed against Edward in 1296 were ready to try again. Wishart and James the Stewart had plucked up their courage and with Robert Bruce, grandson of the Competitor and the future king, were in rebellion independently of Wallace. Douglas, from the vicinity of Perth where he had been with Wallace, joined with them, as did others. This aristocratic uprising did not endure. The participants were not sustained by a singlemindedness similar to Wallace's. If it is unnecessary to disparage their motives, we may question their dedication. Wishart and James the Stewart were not without courage but were not in military terms heroic figures. Their strength was in political manoeuvring. Bruce, although Barrow's defence of him is, as always, authoritative,[46] cannot easily be cleared of the charge that his cause was always Bruce. Unlike his father who remained faithful to the English king who so despised him, Bruce was not unworthy of the English suspicions to which the bishop of Carlisle gave expression.[47]

The English had no difficulty in dealing with the Scots. Already in June, Henry Percy, grandson of Edward's viceroy Surrey, and Robert Clifford, a member of the great Westmorland family, had received their instructions from Edward.[48] The two were to 'arrest, imprison, and 'justify' all disturbers of the peace in Scotland'. Cressingham was 'to give his personal aid and counsel' to the northerners. Percy and Clifford did not delay. Perhaps in part motivated by the knowledge that any success by the Scots might lead to an invasion of the north of England with consequent effects upon their own lands, they gathered levies in the Border counties and by the end of June were at Ayr.[49] In choosing to move against Bruce, the Stewart, and Wishart, Percy and Clifford achieved much at little expense. They had no difficulty in facing down the Scots lords who surrendered to them at Irvine (see Chapter 4) without striking a blow.

NOTES

1. *Scalacronicon*, 17.

2. It is Cressingham who is generally considered the more arrogant of the two. Certainly, he was not spared in the chronicles, e.g. Guisborough, 294, 302, 303. His birth may have counted against him. Surrey had no such excuse for his arrogance towards the Scots.

3. Prestwich, 50: 'Edward's successes were achieved as a result of well-organised logistics, not by tactical or strategic skill'. For Edward's wars consult principally J.E. Morris, e.g. *The Welsh Wars of Edward I*, 1901; *Bannockburn*, 1914, chap. 3 entitled 'Tactics before Bannockburn'. For a more specialised aspect of the war with Scotland see his article, 'Mounted Infantry in Medieval Warfare', *Trans. Cumb. & West. Ant. & Arch. Soc.* 23 April 1914.

4. Barron, 77.

5. We are in any case left to guess what Barron meant by the term 'an army'.

6. Barrow, *Robert Bruce*, 216, writes of Methven as 'a rout rather than a battle'.

7. Guisborough, 294.

8. *Ibid.*

9. Guisborough, 303.

10. Barron, chaps. 3-6 has the fullest account of these uprisings.

11. Lanercost, Maxwell translation, 122.

12. Barrow: *Robert Bruce*, 114. See also Barrow: *Kingdom of the Scots*, chap. 8 and Barron, 24-25 on the role of the Scottish Church in general in the war.

13. Guisborough, 299.

14. Lanercost, Maxwell translation, 163.

15. He was peculiarly inconsistent in his attitude, however, as his behaviour on the raid into England in 1297 indicates, particularly in the famous incident at Hexham. See below, chap. 5.

16. Barrow: *Robert Bruce*, 115.

17. See Powicke, 684 and note on Wishart's somewhat equivocal stance in 1297.

18. As Wallace was associated with Wishart, so was Murray with his uncle, David of Moravia, who became bishop of Moray in 1299. For the bishop, see Barrow: *Kingdom of the Scots*, 238-9.

19. Barron, 32-57 contains the story in some detail of Andrew Murray's work.

20. *Cal. Docs. Scot.*, ii, 742.

21. Barron, 33.

22. *Cal. Docs. Scot.*, ii, 922.

23. *Ibid.*, 922, 931.

24. Stevenson (ed.), *Documents Illustrative of the History of Scotland, 1288-1306*, ii, 212.

25. Guisborough, 297.

26. Of Rait Castle, near Nairn. He was a neighbour of Andrew Murray.

27. q. Barron, 56.

28. Guisborough, 297, expresses similar suspicions.

29. August 5, 1297.

30. See below, Chapter 4.

31. McNair Scott, 39.

32. Barrow: *Robert Bruce*, 117n. argues the case most convincingly for this spelling in preference to any other.

33. Sixth Book.

34. *Ibid.*

35. *Ibid.*
36. Seventh Book.
37. See below, chap. 10, for the indictment.
38. Edward, in the indictment, mentioned an offer of pardon after Falkirk. Presumably this included the murder.
39. Barbour: *Bruce,* 24.
40. Guisborough, 295.
41. On Fordun, the reader is referred to the introductory note to the Select Bibliography.
42. Rishanger, 373.
43. *Cal. Docs. Scot.,* ii, 357, 358, 365, 429, 431, 468.
44. Guisborough, 295.
45. *Ibid.*
46. Barrow: *Robert Bruce,* 119ff.
47. Guisborough, 295.
48. *Cal. Docs. Scot,* ii, 887.
49. Guisborough, 297-8.

CHAPTER 4

The Time of Revenge, 1297-1298

Wallace shared with the great commanders of history the ability to recognise and take advantage of an opportunity.[1] He was now, in July 1297, to be presented with a crucial opening. Irvine, albeit in a negative sense, marked a significant stage in his public career, perhaps more so even than Lanark. He was, as always, swift to profit from it.

Wallace and Andrew Murray, alone of the Scottish principals in the events of that summer, were untainted by the fiasco of Irvine. It is not clear whether, like Douglas, Wallace had ridden south to join with Bruce and the others. If present at all during the preliminary manoeuvrings,[2] he had left, it may be guessed in disgust, before the capitulation to Percy and Clifford on 7 July.[3] The failure of nerve of the Scots leaders had one interesting consequence which may help us to understand Wallace's own attitude to his colleagues. So distressed was he by the behaviour of Bruce, Wishart, and the Stewart, that Sir Richard Lundie switched to the English side.[4] He was a useful acquisition.[5] That contemporary criticism of the Scots leadership cannot be discounted. It is impossible to believe that others did not share his despair, even if they did not at this point defect with him. His action has, however, been balanced by a more sympathetic view of those he had criticised, and a different role suggested for them. Thus a connection has been drawn between the undoubtedly protracted negotiations with the English at Irvine and the freedom these same negotiations offered to Wallace.[6] That the Scots had a definite purpose in prolonging the talks with Percy and Clifford appears to be the opinion of at least one English chronicler. For him the link with Wallace is evident: 'And there [i.e. at Irvine], day after day slipped by in timewasting bickerings and argument, while that bandit Wallace gathered the people to him . . . By now, indeed, he had raised an immense army'.[7]

Wallace was extremely active in the month after the surrender at Irvine.[8] To see in him one who was in any part of a plot hatched before Irvine stretches the imagination. He is more likely to have gone ahead with his own plans in contempt of the other leaders in the west. His vigour contrasts starkly with their hesitation. One factor must not be overlooked in the light of their future attitude to him. They were intent upon protecting their position and their lands, something denied to Wallace who because of the murder of Heselrig was an outlaw. They were, at Irvine as ever, both more realistic and self-seeking than he was or became.[9] By seeking terms on 7 July,[10] they must have enraged if not yet alienated Wallace. His reaction to the disgrace at Irvine was a sharp raid on Wishart's palace at Ancrum.[11] From there he carried away not only a number of the bishop's possessions but also his sons who are, perhaps for reasons of delicacy, referred to as his nephews. But the grudge which the raid suggests he bore against Wishart did not last.

Percy and Clifford, surprisingly, did not immediately trade upon their defeat of the Scots. Wallace can only have been encouraged by this. Percy and Clifford do not appear to have been averse to the period of relaxation which the negotiations allowed them. Having defeated the Scots in the simplest of ways, they were, understandably but mistakenly, somewhat smug. The martial determination of the Irvine campaign had lapsed, as Cressingham indicates in a letter of 23 July to Edward.[12] He was himself not without military pretensions, and his account of recent developments is informative. He represents himself as bent upon action against the Scots while the victors of Irvine will not move, he tells his king, until the arrival of the dilatory Surrey at Berwick. It is from this letter that we learn that Wallace, 'with a large company', was in the Forest of Selkirk.[13] Cressingham was already describing Wallace to Edward as 'like one who holds himself against your peace'. It is a revealing and accurate phrase. For Cressingham, rather more perceptive than his English colleagues, not to mention certain of the Scots, Wallace was not waiting upon events or orders.

Such was not, of course, Wallace's nature. Once his mind was made up, and he was far from rash in making it up, he acted forcefully and with dispatch. Thus, there is no evidence that in July 1297, or indeed at any time until after he had resigned the Guardianship in the next year, he allowed his conduct to be dictated by his ostensible superiors. If he had ever been subservient, other than in the purely formal sense, to the likes of Wishart and the Stewart, that had passed with the murder of Heselrig. It is therefore possible that it is from the summer of 1297 that we may trace the animosity of the Scots lords to him. Wallace's inherent aggressiveness, in the personal and military senses, cut across preconceptions of what was fitting. He acted on his own judgement. This cannot have endeared him to Bruce or later to Comyn, any more than it did to Edward. These three, even when enemies, shared a common heritage from which Wallace was excluded. A later comment may help us to understand his relations with the Scots nobility.[14] Having been regaled with a list of Wallace's virtues, we are told: 'Gaining strength daily, he in a short time, by force, and by dint of his prowess, brought all the magnates of Scotland under his sway, whether they would or not. Some of the magnates, moreover, as did not thankfully obey his commands, he took and browbeat, and handed over to custody, until they should utterly submit to his good pleasure. And when all had thus been subdued, he manfully betook himself to the storming of castles and fortified towns in which the English ruled; for he aimed at quickly and thoroughly freeing his country and overthrowing the enemy'.

It is easy to detect in this passage the prejudice of the writer. We are required to believe that not until he had mastered the forces within Scotland itself which hindered independence was he able to turn his attention to the English. A fifth column, to use a more modern expression, had to be eliminated. The existence of this hostile section is a matter for debate, of course. It is also true that what we read relates to the period of Wallace's ascendancy, when because of the Guardianship he had absolute authority. Yet we can recognise here the Wallace of the summer of 1297. He was already distinguished by his singlemindedness. It led him into that kind of ruthlessness of which we have read.[15] He did not scruple to force fellow-Scots, of whatever station, to obey him in the war against England.

An interesting example of Wallace's attitude is to be found in the case of Michael de Miggel.[16] In September 1305, a month after Wallace's execution, Michael was called to explain his conduct at Perth before, among others, Malise earl of Strathearn, and sir Malcolm de Inverpefray. To them he related his treatment at Wallace's hands. He claimed that he had twice escaped from Wallace and that, recaptured, he had survived only through the intervention of some of Wallace's men. Wallace relented but warned him that a third attempt at escape would mean death. Aware no doubt of the danger in which his unwilling association with Wallace placed him, Michael pleaded that 'he remained with William through fear of death and not of his own will'. Fortunately for him, his story was believed. Edward, who with the death of Wallace seemed to have become more reasonable, ordered that Michael's goods and chattels were to be restored to him.[17] There is no reason to suppose that Michael de Miggel was in any way unique in having been dragooned into service by Wallace.[18]

If this is indeed so, two questions pose themselves. Firstly, who in Wallace's eyes was the enemy? The answer must be that he regarded as such not merely the English who occupied his country but also any who did not identify themselves, to his satisfaction, as actively hostile to the English. It was a simplistic, and dangerous, stance to take. It demonstrated an ignorance of, or perhaps an indifference to, the realities of political life and, finally, it undid him. There can be no doubt, however, that in the circumstances of the summer of 1297, it was the only position for one with his intentions and temperament.

That brings us to the second question: what was Wallace trying to do at this time? If the answer is obvious – to rid Scotland of English rule and to restore Balliol – it is not complete. Wallace was intelligent enough to realise that to expel the English from Scotland would not of itself restore Balliol to the throne. Such a restoration, being essentially a political matter, was not something of which Wallace was capable in the summer of 1297, although he remained dedicated to the idea. He was, however, able to inflict on the English enemy such blows as they had not yet suffered. In this connection a consideration of his actions after Irvine is instructive.

As has been seen from Cressingham's letter of 23 July, Wallace was based on the Forest of Selkirk. At the same time, Cressingham was telling Edward how desperate the situation, from the English standpoint, had become: 'By far the greater part of your counties in the Scottish kingdom are still not provided with helpers, because they have been killed, besieged, or imprisoned, or have abandoned their bailiwicks and dare not go back. And in some shires the Scots have appointed and established bailiffs and officials. Thus no shire is properly kept save for Berwick and Roxburgh-shire, and they only recently'.[19]

It has been argued that Wallace alone could not be responsible for the conditions which Cressingham was describing.[20] In that he had certainly not taken into his hands the reins of government, the argument is correct. The authority he enjoyed was still military rather than political; there was no question of his being endowed with the Guardianship at this period. But who other than he on the Scottish side had the name, backed by success, to inspire the reversal portrayed by Cressingham? The Scottish officials who are referred to by the treasurer were not and could not be Wallace's creation. We are therefore speaking of their resuming a role with which they had been familiar under Balliol. Nevertheless, they could not have resumed that role unaided. Wallace, by his actions and his example, made that possible.

He had with him in the Forest of Selkirk a large following. He made no effort, to our knowledge, to move with it against the English who, as Cressingham's letter of 23 July makes clear, were waiting for their commander, Surrey, to arrive.[21] That Wallace did not do so is important. Given the use he made of intelligence, he might very well have thought that an attack on the English, leaderless and gathering as they were, was worthwhile. If he considered that possibility, he did not act upon it. Instead, as we know, he turned north and east from Selkirk. Blind Harry has him reach Aberdeen,[22] where he burned a hundred English ships.

Time and distance combine to make this, as is true of so much of what Harry tells us, impossible. Wallace, however, did move rapidly. He swept across Perthshire and Fife, clearing them of the English, and in early August began the siege of Dundee castle.[23]

Cressingham refers to the size of Wallace's army. As the latter's progress proves, it can have been an army in name only; he would have been hindered rather than helped in what he did by large numbers. There is another factor to be considered. A strong rumour current in the summer of 1297 must have contributed both to the numbers and the dubious quality of many who came to him in the Forest of Selkirk. It was the intention of the English king, according to the rumour, 'to seize all the middle folk of Scotland to send them overseas in his war [i.e. with France], to their great damage and destruction'.[24] We cannot confirm the truth of this rumour. But the Scots had reason perhaps to be afraid. With the conquest of Scotland, as he imagined, complete, Edward had already taken with him a number of Scots lords as he prepared for his campaign against Philip IV. The exactions of his officials under Cressingham supported the argument that he looked upon Scotland as a fief, to be used as he thought suitable, its people therefore at his disposal.[25] However anxious to serve under Wallace in the light of this threat to their freedom, not all who believed the rumour can have been skilled soldiers. They required training and discipline, qualities which he had succeeded in instilling in them by the time of Falkirk. They would not be competent to accompany him as he moved north in the weeks after Lanark. When put to the test at Stirling in September, the larger army which he then used had a different role, one which depended upon Wallace's ability to improvise.

The force which he led out of the Forest of Selkirk must have been only part of the 'immense army' of which Cressingham wrote. Wallace, interestingly, was returning across the Forth to an area with which, both in fact and in fiction, he was familiar. It was here that he had struck in that raid which had almost resulted in the capture of Ormsby. That exploit, it has been noted, required horses, and it is possible that, two months later, he was again at the head of a force largely if not entirely mounted. Mobility was essential if he was to carry out his plan of harassment of the English. He would be unwilling to be hampered, in this undertaking, by any great mass of infantry. The nature of any occupation of a country is that it can never be complete. Key centres are used for the purpose of local government, castles held, the network of roads dominated. Wallace, like Murray, knew this, hence his strategy. Part of his force must have been professional, composed of soldiers owing their first loyalty to the great feudal figures, such as the Stewart and Robert Bruce. Their presence with Wallace may be proof of the most valuable contribution that the magnates themselves, found wanting first at Dunbar then at Irvine, could make at this time to the cause which Wallace now personified.

If Wallace had detached part of the army of the Forest of Selkirk with the intention of harassing the English north of the Forth, another consequence followed. It drew the English army at Berwick, with Surrey at last at its head, away from the secure base which that town offered. Surrey was at first no more willing than before to stir himself.[26] He was no longer young, less than enthusiastic about the war in Scotland, and would therefore be far from disappointed when, on 18 August, he was recalled. He was to join Edward on the Continent. To take his place as keeper of Scotland Brian Fitzalan of Bedale was nominated. Surrey's replacement was a man of considerable experience of Scottish affairs, having been made a Guardian by Edward I as early as June of 1291.[27] Fitzalan was, however, very conscious that he was not a wealthy man. Unless that unfortunate situation was remedied, he reasoned, he felt unable to accept the honour which Edward held out to him. The king, with heavy commitments, sensed an opportunity to use the change of command to reduce both Fitzalan's salary and the forces available to him. He rejected Fitzalan's argument. The lethargic and indifferent Surrey was to remain in command in Scotland.[28]

The contrast between Surrey and Cressingham, the one less than eager, the other, if we can rely on his own words, pressing for an early engagement with the Scots, did not augur well for the English army as it advanced from Berwick. It is doubtful if either understood the threat which Wallace, the new man, posed. Surrey had learned his trade as a soldier in the baronial wars of the reign of Henry III, some thirty years previously. His success at Dunbar in 1296, if important, did not prepare him for what faced him now. Cressingham, lacking the advantages which his nominal superior enjoyed from birth, was both impatient for and intent on advancement through solving the problem of Scotland.[29] It was a fateful liaison. They did, however, share a contempt for the enemy. Surrey, for so long absent if not in hiding in England, did not have the advantage of direct involvement in the rapidly changing situation of the country for which he held responsibility. Cressingham, who did have that advantage, was as conservative as the other when it came to the means of dealing with the resurgent Scots. Neither appears to have been in the slightest doubt that the Scots, lately humiliated at Irvine, would once again be readily trounced by the traditional use of the English army.

The size of that army eludes us. As always, we turn in vain to the contemporary chronicles if we hope for accuracy. Guisborough, even if able to draw on the experience of a participant, Sir Marmaduke de Tweng, cannot be cleared of exaggeration. Tweng was a veteran soldier who later fell into Wallace's hands but survived to fight and be captured at Bannock-burn; he would hardly be the source, as has been suggested,[30] of the figure which Guisborough gives.[31] One thousand horse and fifty thousand foot are nicely rounded numbers but debateable. Wiser perhaps, Lanercost, eschewing the need to be precise, is content with a reference to 'a great army'.[32] This vague but suitably impressive description was to be echoed by Fordun. We may come nearer to the truth if we revert to the letters of Cressingham in the search for some approximation of accuracy. The treasurer, whose industry in reporting to his king is quite remarkable, had no cause to distort the numbers of those at his disposal when he wrote to Edward on 23 July. He stated that he had mustered at Roxburgh three hundred horse and ten thousand foot.[33] This was for the time, after all, a not inconsiderable force, one which bears comparison with those on either side at the majority of battles with which we are most familiar.[34] To Cressingham and Surrey, both assuming the outcome guaranteed, it would have seemed more than adequate for the purpose.

When we turn to the numbers of the Scottish army which would face them at Stirling we are no better informed. That army was the joint responsibility of Wallace and Andrew Murray, each of whom had brought contingents. The exact numbers with each of the two are not recorded, nor is there any way of measuring the proportion of foot to horse soliders. If, like Wallace, Murray had relied on cavalry to give him success against the English, he, again like Wallace, would have recourse to infantry in the forthcoming battle. Cressingham and Surrey had reached Stirling by the first week in September. At some date before this Wallace and Murray, whose respective campaigns were so similar, had met and at once had discovered an affinity which caused them to realise the advantages of a single opposition to the English. We cannot suppose that their meeting was accidental. Each would have known of the other; their successes were based on the same strategy, and that strategy depended upon good intelligence. It is possible that they met at Dundee which Wallace was besieging. If so, the date may have been on or about 8 September. Lanercost informs us that it was at this date, the Nativity of the Glorious Virgin, that 'they [i.e. the Scots] began to show themselves in rebellion'. It is a strange remark in the light of what had gone before; it may reflect a later view that the decision to fight the army led by Surrey and Cressingham was taken then. Since Wallace and Murray were at the head of the Scots at Stirling, the chronicle may be referring to them. In any case Wallace and Murray would have been in no doubt as to the destination of the English.

The strategic importance of the castle of Stirling, overlooking the crossing of the Forth, was as clear to them as to the English.

Fordun casts an interesting light on the actions of Wallace as he moved from Dundee to Stirling. Wallace, he tells us, learned of the advance of the English and at once got ready to march to Stirling. Before setting out, however, he 'entrusted the care and charge of the castle to the burgesses of that town [Dundee] on pain of loss of life and limb'. Here again we have, if the evidence is correct, an example of Wallace's ruthlessness. He appears to have had no hesitation in employing threats in pursuit of his aims. We know him to have been a harsh man, but why was it necessary, once again, to browbeat those who ought to have been his allies? The incident tells us, perhaps, more about the attitude of adherents to the Scottish cause than about Wallace himself. The good folk of Dundee were alive to the possibility of retribution if Wallace, the hero of the moment, failed at Stirling. They cannot have been unique in their uncertainty.

The battle of Stirling was fought on 11 September. It was preceded by an intriguing intervention on the part of certain Scots nobles. The English reached the Forth in the first week of the month. On 9 September James the Stewart and Malcolm earl of Lennox at the head of other nobles approached Surrey with the offer of arbitrating with the Scots who were stationed on the Abbey Craig. If Cressingham, as seems possible, demurred, Surrey was more agreeable. We can only guess at the motives of the nobles and whether they made a genuine attempt to carry out their promise. According to Lanercost, the Stewart at least was guilty of treachery. A more modern view suggests that the Stewart and his companions hoped to avert a slaughter of the Scots.[35] If they approached Wallace, he would not be of a mood to put faith in them; Irvine was too close. The lords, in any case, returned to Surrey the next day to confess failure. Perhaps as a sop, they undertook to join him on the eleventh with forty knights.

As the lords left the English camp, an incident occurred which demonstrated the volatile nature of the situation. Guisborough tells what happened in these terms:

'As they [i.e. the Scots] were leaving our camp that evening, they met a band of our returning foragers and began abusing them, and Lennox wounded a foot-soldier in the neck with his sword. When this was known to our army, everyone hurried to arm themselves, and they brought the wounded and bleeding man before the Earl of Warenne, crying out that vengeance should be taken that very night.

'But the earl replied, 'Let us wait tonight, and see whether they keep their promise in the morning; then we shall better be able to demand satisfaction for this insult'".

Surrey's quaint belief in the knightly right to reply is faintly ridiculous to us. It is as incomprehensible as the exact role of the Scots lords. Wallace, as has been suggested, can have had no faith in them. They may, despite this, have acted after a discussion with him and Murray; the two commanders would not be unwilling to benefit from any delay which the lords could gain for them. It is difficult to believe that Lennox and the Stewart could hope to assume command of the Scots army, even if they had the courage. This was the time of Wallace and Murray. The lords did in the event have a further part to play in the battle of Stirling, but it was a minor one and far from heroic. Their force of cavalry was allocated no function in the plan which Wallace and Murray employed on 11 September. That plan appears to have been largely improvised, and was the work of men of a different mentality from the lords'. It is noteworthy, nevertheless, that the contemporary accounts of the battle lay such emphasis on the involvement of the lords. If noteworthy, it is not surprising; we sense that the chroniclers are no more able to give credit to Wallace than they were in describing what had happened at Lanark.

On the evening of 10 September, having allowed the Scots lords to depart, Surrey had informed his officers that the army would cross the bridge the following morning. Amazingly, he slept in. Before he rose, the army began the crossing. In the account in Guisborough, from which so much of our information comes, some five thousand infantry had reached the other side of the bridge. As it was capable of taking only two men abreast, this manoeuvre could not be speedy. Wallace and Murray, with a coolness remarkable in the circumstances, held fast on the Abbey Craig. The temptation to attack the English must have been great but it was resisted. In their restraint it is possible to see the implementation of a scheme, which was at length put into effect. This, of course, is the accepted view. In this, Wallace and Murray intended from the beginning to throw their army down on the English as they crossed the bridge. If that is so, one wonders why they did not take this first opportunity. That they did not then launch the onslaught makes it likely that they had not yet decided to fight at all. Thus, they watched and waited. That part of the English army which had crossed did not remain over the bridge; it was recalled because Surrey had not yet risen. This failure of the English to consolidate their hold on the river bank was a piece of good fortune for Wallace and Murray. If it is indeed true that five thousand infantry had made the crossing, that was a formidable force; it would have given the two commanders pause. The outcome of the battle might have been different, if indeed an engagement had taken place at all.

What was already, from the English point of view, farcical, grew worse.

In keeping with his somewhat inappropriate code of honour, Surrey insisted on creating several new knights. Of these, Guisborough dolefully tells us, 'many were to fall that day'. Surrey then ordered the crossing to begin. Once more those who had gone forward were called back, for it was seen that the Stewart and Lennox, set on a place in history, were returning. They had not brought with them the forty horsemen they had promised. This was interpreted as a good sign; the Scots, Surrey thought, were come to surrender. On the contrary, the lords had come to confess failure. As Guisborough relates, 'they only made excuses, saying they could neither persuade their followers to submit nor even obtain horses or weapons from them'. Quite who these followers were we can only guess. If it is a reference to Wallace and Murray, it is ludicrous, since they were in no sense followers. If a mention of the retinue of the lords, their numbers were hardly sufficient to be of consequence in the battle to come.

Surrey was not yet done with talking. Despite the threat which Wallace and Murray posed from the height of the Abbey Craig, despite the admitted futility of the endeavours of the Scots lords and their brief but vicious treachery of the night before, he was not ready to fight. To Wallace and Murray he sent two Dominican friars. In Guisborough it is, noticeably, Wallace not Murray who is credited with a terse but famous rejoinder to Surrey's demand for surrender: 'Tell your commander that we are not here to make peace but to do battle to defend ourselves and liberate our kingdom. Let them come on, and we shall prove this in their very beards'.[36]

These splendid remarks do not, given the time at which they were uttered, invalidate the argument that Wallace and Murray were not at first intent upon giving battle. They had seen the various actions of Surrey's army, they knew of the approaches made by the Scots lords even if they did not necessarily approve of them; they knew now that they had nothing to fear. Their confidence was well placed. Below them the English, having failed to achieve a second Irvine, were at odds. That same Sir Richard Lundie who, angry and disgusted, had left the Scots camp at Irvine, put the case for caution: 'My lords, if we cross that bridge now, we are all dead men. For we can only go over two abreast, and the enemy are already formed up: they can charge down on us whenever they wish'.

Lundie foresaw what was to happen. Wallace and Murray were stationed on the southward-looking slope of the Abbey Craig at a distance to the north of one mile from the bridge over which the English, some of them for the third time, were preparing to cross. Between the foot of the Abbey Craig and the northern end of the bridge was a causeway which ran over soft ground unsuitable for the heavy cavalry on which Surrey's army relied for impact, both physical and psychological. Once the English had crossed, not only would it be difficult if not impossible to deploy the cavalry, but the infantry would be surrounded on three sides by the river as it formed a horseshoe loop. Lundie understood the double danger offered by Wallace and Murray; even if the crossing were unimpeded by the Scots – an unlikely eventuality – the chances of Surrey's being able so to order his deployment in the face of an attack which would then, if not before, occur, were slight. Lundie, therefore, proposed that a detachment under his command move along the river and set upon Wallace and Murray from the rear. 'There is', he told Surrey, 'a ford not far from here, where sixty men can cross at a time. Give me five hundred cavalrymen, then, and a small body of infantry, and we will outflank the enemy and attack them from behind: while we are doing that, the earl and the rest of the army will be able to cross the bridge in perfect safety'.

If Lundie's advice had been heeded, the outcome of the battle of Stirling must have been different. Wallace and Murray would have been forced to divide their army and would have lost the opportunity to attack the English, as they crossed the bridge, with sufficient strength. But if Surrey had lost the first and perhaps best opening by calling back those troops who had established themselves over the river before he had risen from his bed, he now made another gross mistake. He allowed Cressingham, who had not so far been prominent, to intervene. The treasurer urged an immediate crossing and an attack upon the Scots. It was natural that Cressingham should be concerned about the cost of keeping an army in the field; he it was who had sent men home to England on the grounds of expense. He now used the same argument in support of the crossing. He rounded on Surrey who seemed about to agree with Lundie: 'It will do us no good, my lord earl, either to go bickering like this or to waste the king's money by vain manoeuvres. So let us cross over right away, and do our duty as we are bound to do'. If Cressingham was a fool, his superior, Surrey, was even worthier of the title. He overruled Lundie and ordered the advance. For Lundie it is impossible not to feel sympathy. If the Scots at Irvine had lacked courage, the English at Stirling lacked intelligence. The words of Guisborough might well be his own: 'Thus (amazing though it is to relate, and terrible as was to be its outcome) all these experienced men, though they knew the enemy was at hand, began to pass over a bridge so narrow that even two horsemen could scarcely and with much difficulty ride side by side – and so they did all the morning, without let or hindrance, until the vanguard was on one side of the river and the remainder of the army on the other. There was, indeed, no better place in all the land to deliver the English into the hands of the Scots, and so many into the power of the few'.

What happened appears to us, with the benefit of hindsight, inevitable.

Wallace and Murray watched the parade of the English on to the bridge. With that fine judgement which marks the exceptional commander, they released their infantry down the slope of Abbey Craig when the vanguard of the English army had almost made the crossing. The Scots, their patience rewarded, fell upon the vanguard as it attempted to debouch from the bridge. The vanguard was now cut off from the rest of the English army which was forced to watch from the far bank. The narrowness of the bridge made any move to reinforce those unfortunates already over the bridge impossible. Wallace and Murray had with part of their force blocked the northern end of the bridge. What the larger part of the English army saw was horrifying.

The Scots in the rush down from the Abbey Craig would have gathered an immense momentum. This must have driven many of the English off the bank and into the river. Such as escaped this fate cannot have had time to offer any kind of concerted opposition. Their superior weapons could not be brought to bear in the crush. Retreat was impossible. One English version of events has Wallace break the bridge down at this point. Whether this is so, or whether Warenne, who had not crossed the bridge, had it destroyed to save himself and the larger part of the army, we do not know, but it did not matter. The Scots made great slaughter of the vanguard. A hundred knights and many infantry, perhaps as many as five thousand, died, either killed or drowned.

Among those who perished was Cressingham. If Surrey had not crossed the bridge, the treasurer had been less prudent. He had charged at the head of the vanguard, his mind no doubt filled with the dreams of that glory which the office of treasurer had denied him. Misguided, pompous, less than popular with his own army, he nevertheless met the sort of end which was more appropriate to such as Surrey. He was dragged down from his horse and died under the spears of the Scots infantry. In telling of his death, Guisborough does not spare him: 'Of all the many who were deceived that day, he was deceived most of all'. After the battle, the Scots, in a gruesome ceremony, flayed his obese body. Strips of his skin were sent throughout Scotland to proclaim the victory of Stirling. Other strips were used to make saddle girths. Wallace himself had a belt made for his sword from what was left of Cressingham's skin.

Of those who escaped from the massacre, some swam the river. These were Welshmen who fought as always without armour. The most famous of those who did survive was Sir Marmaduke de Tweng, the Yorkshireman. He refused to joint the Welshmen as they swam the river and rode his horse through the Scots and over the bridge to safety. He, clearly, had seen the hopelessness of the situation very early, for the bridge was still intact.

His courage and his continued devotion to the English Crown, first in the person of Edward I and then in that of the king's son, ensured that his reputation did not suffer. The same could not be said of Surrey. He gave Stirling Castle into Tweng's keeping and fled for Berwick with unseemly haste.

There was a postscript to the battle. We left the Stewart and the earl of Lennox after their report to Surrey on the refusal of Wallace and Murray to surrender. Now with the battle over and Surrey in flight, they reappeared on the scene. They had been spectators of the slaughter at the river, and it is not certain what use, if any, they had made of their men. Their target now was the English baggage-train, the camp-followers, and other refugees from the battle. These were moving in the direction of Falkirk when the lords emerged from the shelter of the woods alongside The Pows and fell upon them. Many of the English were killed and large amounts of booty seized. It was the sole contribution of the Stewart and Lennox to the Scottish achievement of Stirling.

NOTES

1. For Machiavelli (*op. cit.*, 202) this attribute ranked highest in the rules of military discipline. Clausewitz deals with the question, *op. cit.*, book 1, chap. 3.

2. If Wallace was present, it is difficult to see in what role. He could only have been there as the leader of an independent force gathered since Lanark or in the Stewart's following. In neither case is there mention of him. Had he been present, his departure would surely have been noted, especially if there had been a quarrel leading to that departure.

3. *Cal. Docs. Scot.*, ii, 908.

4. Lundie fought for the English at Stirling. See above, pp. 53-54, for the part he played.

5. Trivet, 357, describes him as '*miles strenuus*'.

6. Barrow: *Robert Bruce*, 120-121. Mackay: *Robert Bruce King of Scots*, 1974, 62, sees the Stewart as particularly responsible for the tactic. Barron, 46, states categorically that the Scots 'had been compelled to make peace'.

7. Guisborough, 299.

8. As late as 5 August, Wishart, Bruce, and the Stewart were still, for whatever reasons, haggling over terms with the English: Barrow: *Robert Bruce*, 120n. Douglas, surely in some respects a man of Wallace's own temperament, having failed to provide hostages, was a prisoner, first at Berwick, where he continued to be 'very savage and abusive', then in the Tower of London, where he died the next year. The Scots believed that he had been murdered.

9. It is fair to state that Bruce, at least, was in a difficult position in the negotiations. He was required to give his daughter, Marjorie, as a hostage. He was, understandably, reluctant and Wishart, with certain others, stood as a guarantor until he should produce Marjorie. *Cal. Docs. Scot.*, ii, 910.

10. Wishart was not named among those who 'confessed their rebellion' on 9 July. *Cal. Docs. Scot.*, ii, 909.

11. Guisborough, 299.

12. *Cal. Docs. Scot.*, ii, 453. Cressingham had been instructed on 24 June to 'hold a colloquy with Percy and Clifford on the situation'. *Cal. Pat. Rolls, 1292-1301*, 251.

13. On the significance of the forest or 'Greenwood' in outlaw legend, see Keen, 1-8.

14. Fordun, 98.

15. A different interpretation is placed on this aspect of Wallace's methods by *D.N.B.* There, 564, we read that Wallace 'showed wisdom by associating with himself, when possible, representatives of those barons who encouraged by his success, supported him for at least a time'. We are, however, left, even here, to draw the conclusion that the arrangement on Wallace's side did not exclude harsh means, while the nobles, for their part, were ready to withdraw the support which he forced from some of them.

16. Michael de Miggel was captured by the English at Dunbar and imprisoned in Nottingham castle. *Cal. Docs. Scot.*, ii, 742. He was still there on September 23, 1299, when arrangements were being made for him to be exchanged with James de Lindsey, then in Bothwell Castle. *Cal. Docs. Scot.*, ii, 1093. None of this, his endeavours on behalf of the Scottish cause in the early part of the war, the suffering which he underwent in an English prison, seemed, if Michael is to be believed, to weigh with Wallace.

17. *Cal. Docs. Scot.*, ii, 1689.

18. If the case of Michael de Miggel is not unique, it is interesting that there is no record that the execution of Wallace was followed by a rush of people anxious to dissociate themselves from him. The nobles, of course, had already made their peace with Edward and were collaborating with the English.

19. *Cal. Docs. Scot.*, ii, 455.

20. Barrow: *Robert Bruce*, 121.

21. It was not until 1 August that Surrey reached Berwick.

22. Seventh Book. Barron, 60-2, argues that Harry confuses Wallace with Murray and that it was the latter who was at Aberdeen, joining with Henry de Lathom, the English sheriff of Aberdeen, who had gone over to the Scots.

23. Bower, ii, 171.

24. *Docs. Illus. Hist. Scot.*, ii, 198.

25. Edward neglected no source for the levying of troops. On 11 April 1298, for example, he invited 'criminals and vagrants' to serve with him. *Cal. Docs. Scot.*, ii, 38. Geoffrey Entredens, pardoned because of his service in the Scottish war, was but one of many guilty of 'homicides, robberies, and outlawry' and other assorted crimes before Edward offered them a kind of respectability. *Cal. Pat. Rolls*, 199. The effects of such a policy of recruitment may be seen both at Stirling and Falkirk. In the latter case, it came close to bringing defeat for the English king when he found he could not rely on the Welsh contingent in his army.

26. He had, in fact, been ordered to resume his appointment in Scotland on 14 June. Edward's continued confidence in this unwilling warrior is not easy to explain. It was disastrous at Stirling, yet Edward did not dismiss Surrey. For a man of such reputation as a soldier, Edward did not show himself more astute than his son and successor. Edward II, at least, was capable of wise military appointments, most notably in the case of Andrew de Harcla who, however, made the fatal mistake of recognising his monarch's futility. It was Harcla who inflicted the most serious reverse suffered by Robert I at Carlisle in 1315. Lanercost, 230.

27. On the role of Brian Fitzalan in Scotland there are references in Powicke, 597 and n., 604, 686 and n., & 13n; Barrow: *Robert Bruce*, 49, 50, 108.

28. *Docs. Illust. Hist. Scot.*, ii, 230.

29. He was, however, astute enough not to embark on any adventures against the Scots on his own initiative.

30. Kightly, 164.

31. Guisborough, 301.

32. Maxwell trans. 163.

33. Stevenson, ii, 202.

34. See especially Morris.

35. McNair Scott, 45.

36. Guisborough, 300.

CHAPTER 5

The Time of Power, 1298

Posterity has found that the battle of Stirling was not decisive.[1] In that it did not end the war with England, that was certainly true. But in this it was no different from the other great battles of the Scottish struggle for independence, however bloody they were. After Dunbar and Falkirk, the former a victory of the professional over the amateur, the other accomplished with a great slaughter of Wallace's army, the Scots, seemingly crushed, did not succumb. After Bannockburn, with Edward II revealed at a terrible cost to his men as the incompetent he was militarily as well as politically, it took a further fourteen years to bring peace. The bitter momentum of the war which began in 1296 was not to be so readily halted, the legacy of hatred not so easily forgotten. The personalities and motives of the leading figures – Wallace, Edward I, Bruce, Edward II – were such as to ensure a continuation of the war whatever the current situation. Suffering intensified determination. A reverse led to revival.

But if Stirling was not decisive, its impact on the war and on the psychology of both sides cannot be denied. It was revolutionary in its concept and in its effects, more so even than Bannockburn. The leadership on the Scottish side was of a kind not seen before. Wallace and Murray had broken the canons of warfare as they were then understood; theirs was a challenge to the military establishment both in England and in Scotland itself. Whatever their quarrel, the natural leaders on both sides of the Border shared the same creed. It was no longer possible, after Stirling, to pretend that that creed had survived in its entirety. It is Wallace and Murray who, to modern eyes, appear the professionals. The characteristics which the two commanders exhibited before and during the battle – an appreciation of terrain, selection of position, patience, an iron discipline, improvisation, realistic appraisal and recognition of the moment – were those one would expect to find in their opponents. Wallace and Murray were, after all, in a situation unknown to them: the handling of a large, potentially undisciplined army. Their experience had been of the leadership of small, mobile groups for which success was measured in minor gains. Their confidence verged on brashness; it was justified by events. No one, whether Scots or English, could be ignorant either of their ability or of what the future held in military terms.

Which of the two was the more responsible for Stirling has exercised historians.[2] Underlying the discussion there has been a preference to see in Murray rather than in Wallace the genius which won the battle. The origin of this preference resides in the simple but understandable equation that Murray's presence on the Scots side meant victory, his absence, at Falkirk, defeat. It is a futile argument. Murray's achievement at Stirling, like Wallace's, was shared. The similarities in their campaigns before Stirling are enough to suggest that their relationship was the unique one of two men of contrasting backgrounds who thought alike. We cannot know what if any influence each would have had on the other if Murray had lived. We can say that Wallace continued to demonstrate those same qualities of leadership which he, like Murray, possessed before their historic meeting. Murray's achievement was great, but it is idle to attempt to extend it beyond the obvious point. Wallace had much to do without Murray; that he did it shows him for the man he was.

The wound which Murray had received at Stirling was ultimately fatal.[3] It was not until November, however, that he died, and until that time his name is associated, as will be seen, with that of Wallace. Whether he was able to play an active role must be doubted. The established assumption[4] is that he played such a role, but that assumption may owe more to sentiment than to reality. The colossal impact of Stirling required immediate action if it was not to be lost. It is perhaps significant that it is Wallace who is portrayed as the man who undertook, as it were, the necessary physical labour of benefiting from the victory. We would not expect the seriously wounded Murray to carry out the sweep across the south of Scotland which occurred after Stirling. This obvious fact has not always been sufficiently acknowledged. Murray did not lose his authority because he was incapacitated, but he must have had not merely a different but a less demanding part than his colleague and friend.

Surrey, it will be recalled, had fled the field at Stirling. Tweng, whom he had left, with Sir William FitzWarin, in charge of the castle,[5] could not long hope to hold it. When they surrendered it to Wallace because of a lack of provisions, he showed himself as chivalrous as Bruce, who has always been considered a paragon in this regard. He recognised the courage of Tweng and allowed him to live, as he did FitzWarin. A third man bore the name of Ros. He too Wallace spared, for this was the brother of that Robert de Ros whose defection to the Scots at the beginning of the war had endeared him to the Scots as it endeared him to historians. Wallace was not, then, ignorant of that code by which others laid such store. It was a revealing incident.

Wallace had made no attempt to pursue Surrey, who was so desperate that his horse was allowed no time to eat between Stirling and Berwick and foundered on arrival there. Surrey had reserved his energies for escape rather than for battle. Wallace did, however, strike out for Berwick after the celebrations which, naturally, followed the battle. That town, unwalled because of the economies ordered by Edward which Cressingham had carried out so enthusiastically, now had little strategic value but, perhaps because of its fate under Edward, exercised a continuing fascination for both sides. Its inhabitants expected the worst from the victorious Scots whose bloodlust had not been sated by the carnage of Stirling; such as had not fled into England offered no resistance. The numbers of the force Wallace led to Berwick are not recorded, but it would not be, nor needed to be, large. His intention was in part to underscore his triumph and that of Murray, in part to clear the area of the English. To do so he had to move, as so often in the past, with dispatch. He did not on this occasion cross the Border, although his reputation was now such that the inhabitants of Northumberland sought the safety of Newcastle.

The effects of Stirling were felt throughout Scotland. Dundee castle, from which Wallace had moved to Stirling, surrendered and was placed in the care of Alexander Scrymgeour, one of the many minor figures devoted to the end to the Scottish cause.[6] Edinburgh and Roxburgh fell to the Scots but, as was true of Berwick, their castles remained in the hands of the English.[7] But the capture of these towns and the burning of others south of the Forth[8] was not the main preoccupation of Wallace at this time, however enthusiastically he may have participated in or encouraged these gestures of retribution. His mind was filled with a greater ambition.

Wallace and, as far as know, the ailing Murray, had not lost sight of a primary and dominating concern: the restoration of Balliol. To encompass this it was necessary not only to destroy if possible the military power of the English but to retain, in political terms, the name of Balliol as king of Scots. Stirling had gone some way towards achieving the first; it may be that such was the euphoria in Scotland that it was thought the battle was decisive. Wallace did not share that opinion but, if he worked towards the day when there would be a decisive battle, he turned his attention at the same time to the second aim. This called for other and more demanding qualities than those which had brought success in the recent great battle. At Stirling both Wallace and Murray profited from the innate attributes necessary in war. Now they (and after the death of Murray, Wallace alone) proved they possessed a genius in the political and diplomatic fields.

If Scotland was seized after Stirling with a renewed patriotism and a drive towards unity, it lacked the cohesion which a central government gave. Wallace, in the most revolutionary of his acts, supplied this. It is of him alone now that we must speak. To include Murray, even if, as we shall see, his name was associated with Wallace's, is quite wrong. Murray was in decline; within two months of Stirling he was dead. Wallace was unquestionably the governor of Scotland. To be such required skill and, let it not be forgotten, nerve. He stepped beyond the constraints imposed by his origins. In so doing he saved Scotland from the possibility, in time, of civil war even in the face of a renewed threat from England. At the same time, however, he condemned himself to the hostility of the most influential of his fellow-countrymen as well as, of course, the hatred of Edward I.

One of the effects of Stirling had been the rediscovery by certain of the Scots lords of their patriotism. We saw that once Wallace and Murray had massacred the English vanguard, the Stewart and Lennox emerged both from the woods and their own hesitation to strike a blow for the Scottish cause. They were not alone of their kind. To the north the earl of Buchan, the Comyns, the earl of Strathearn and others were happy to be identified with the Scottish cause. More significant for the future was the reappearance of Robert Bruce, a somewhat mysterious figure after the capitulation of Irvine.[9] He was again active in the south-west. Bruce prompted a retaliatory attack into Annandale of his former opponent, Robert Clifford, some time before Christmas. Clifford killed such Scots as he could lay hands on, burned ten townships, then retreated back into England.[10] Surrey too found the courage which deserted him at Stirling and took Berwick. The English were unwilling to undertake anything of more consequence before their king returned from Flanders. Indeed, Surrey would receive in the following February clear instructions that no major campaign against the Scots was to begin until Edward had returned to take personal command. The slight successes which the Scots lords were achieving in the face of moderate English opposition could lead to over-confidence and with it a renewed determination to take the government upon themselves.

Wallace's seizure of the government therefore ensured unity. If it is difficult now to see an alternative to him,[11] there were undoubtedly others among his contemporaries who thought themselves more suited to the role he henceforth had. The taking into his own hands of the reins of government is evidence, if any were needed, of his courage. It is evidence, also, of his selflessness. Intelligent as he was, he must have been aware of the chance to make himself more than governor. The suggestion must have been put to him. He resisted it. If by resisting the temptation he showed himself to be, as has been argued, 'more conservative than the greater magnates',[12] history has not judged him a failure for that but, rather, a man of honour. To have made himself king would have torn Scotland apart and left it the easiest of preys to Edward. Wallace knew this, fortunately for Scotland.

He was not yet given the obvious title, that of Guardian, by those he had led to victory over the English. Whether he sought it or was offered it and refused it, we do not know. He was careful, first with Murray and then alone, to employ in the documents he issued a formal, accurate description of his station as he saw it. From Haddington on 11 October the two wrote to the mayors and communes of Lübeck and Hamburg. The letter had a double intention. It informed the readers that Scotland, an independent kingdom again, had been won back by battle from the English. It was at the same time in the nature of the reopening of those Scottish trading connections with Germany which had been such a feature of the reign of Alexander III. In this important letter, almost certainly one of many on similar themes, the two commanders referred to themselves as 'Andrew Murray and William Wallace, commanders of the army of the kingdom of Scotland, and the community of that realm'.[13] When in November they issued a letter of. protection to the abbey of Hexham, the formula was no different from that used earlier: 'Andrew Murray and William Wallace, commanders of the army of the kingdom of Scotland, in the name of the famous prince the lord John by God's grace illustrious king of Scotland, by consent of the community of that realm'.[14] With Murray dead, Wallace saw no need to alter the style of greeting, save that he now described himself as knight and Guardian, both titles which he had been given by the time of the grant of a charter to Alexander Scrymgeour. As well as being entrusted with the responsibility for Dundee, Scrymgeour was given land in return for which he was required to pay homage to Balliol and to act as standard bearer to the king. Even at this stage, March of 1298, Wallace, despite a latter claim, had no intention to make himself ruler of Scotland. We can therefore see that he retained, beyond any question, his loyalty to Balliol and held himself to be acting with the agreement of the people of Scotland. That he actively sought both advice and consent is evident from one of the charges brought against him in 1305, that he called 'parliaments and assemblies'. These conferred authority on the actions which he took. No less true, they emphasised his superiority over any pretenders to the position which he had earned since Lanark.

It was as the representative of the Scottish nation that he took an army on an extended raid into the northern counties of England. That nation demanded retribution from the English. It was not a desire from which he dissented. Under him there was in October and November 1297 a return to that savage and indiscriminate kind of warfare with which the Scots had opened the struggle against England. It was, indeed, a long-standing feature of relations between the two countries—and continued to be so for centuries after Wallace—that each side should indulge in destruction and killing for their own sake. Wallace needed neither excuse nor reason for the raid. It was an end in itself. The conduct of his troops, as will be seen, was such as to suggest that Wallace was bent on punishment. It was an emotion which the Scots understood. The need to lead out of a famine-stricken Scotland what must have been a considerable force in the search for sustenance may also have carried some weight.[15] Equally important, however, would be the problem posed by the inactivity of the army of Stirling, successful, enthusiastic, perhaps over-confident. The north of England offered an easy target. The name of Wallace guaranteed a lack of opposition.

Guisborough dates the start of the raid from about 18 October.[16] If that account is to be believed, Wallace struck unexpectedly at Northumberland. Many who had fled into hiding or to the safety of Newcastle when word of Stirling was received, had made their way home. They were now to pay for their folly. The Scots fell upon them, killed as many as could be found and indulged in an orgy of burning and looting. Wallace had his headquarters in the forest of Rothbury. The activities of the Scots were unimpeded by the local population, who thought only of safety. It was thus, we read, that 'the service of God totally ceased in all the monasteries and churches between Newcastle and Carlisle, for all the canons, monks and priests fled before the face of the Scots, as did nearly all the people'. The castles were too strong for Wallace, who had not come prepared for any kind of siege; that was an art which baffled even Bruce at the beginning of his reign.

It is with the Northumberland phase of the raid that a strange incident is associated. At Hexham the priory had not been wholly abandoned. Three canons had come back and were found by a party of the Scots, who called upon them to produce the priory's treasures. The canons answered that everything of value had been stolen by other Scots. At this point Wallace arrived. He felt the need for the services of the canons and asked them to celebrate mass. In keeping with pious practice, he went from the abbey to lay down his arms after the Host had been elevated. In his absence some Scots entered and removed holy articles without which the service could not continue.

When Wallace learned of this, he ordered the capture and hanging of the thieves. A halfhearted attempt was made by the Scots to carry out his instructions. At this Wallace admitted to the canons that the thieves could not really be brought to justice and gave the canons a letter of protection. Barrow compares this incident with a similar one in the reign of David I.[17] That king had hanged men guilty of attempted robbery from the same priory. It is Barrow's view that Wallace's failure to bring thieves to justice proves that, despite his success at Stirling, he had none of the royal authority which David enjoyed. It is no less likely he was wise enough to realise that the volatile Scots would not see the justice in the execution of a number of their comrades for that violence against the English clergy in which they had been encouraged not merely by Wallace but by their own priests. Wallace was not without a sense of what was possible. The propaganda value of his pretence to capture the thieves and, still more to the point, his letter of protection to the canons would not escape him.

Cumberland and Durham felt the anger of the Scots. Wallace's men ranged as far as Cockermouth. At Carlisle, always a challenge and a hurdle to the Scots, he essayed a brief assault, despite his lack of siege equipment. The citizens, as so often in the face of Scottish pretension to the capture of Carlisle, were not impressed. They themselves were well prepared with defensive weapons. Wallace called upon them to surrender. His intermediary was a priest whose words are transmitted to us through the Chronicle of Lanercost, a fact which must cast some doubt on their accuracy. The priest, 'shameless' that he was, cried: 'William the Conqueror, whom I serve, commands you to give up this town and castle without bloodshed; then you may leave unharmed with all your goods. But if you do not instantly obey him, he will attack and kill you all'. Wallace's summons cannot have been serious; he was too hardheaded to believe that surrender would follow. It was a formality, as was his presence, intended to parade before the citizens the army he led as a means of ensuring that no counterattack would be mounted against him. If for his part he could not take this or other fortified places, he guaranteed that there would be no attempt on the part of their garrisons to interfere with his progress through the north of England. Wallace sought no battles on this raid.

The reply of the citizens of Carlisle would not have surprised him. As it is reported to us, it contained no hint of compromise.[18] They dared him to do his worst; they remained faithful to the king who had put the town and castle into their keeping. They were in any case under no illusion as to the temper of Wallace and the Scots; surrender to these men who had slaughtered and burned would not mean safety. They followed up their defiance with a show of the engines of war which stood on the walls of the town. Wallace did not delay at Carlisle; there were other, easier pickings. The Scots vented their spleen on the villages and hamlets which lay within the great forest of Inglewood.

If Wallace was defeated in Cumberland by the walls and castle of Carlisle, he met a far more formidable obstacle when he planned to ravage the county of Durham, which enjoyed the protection of Saint Cuthbert. Wallace's route into Durham was the traditional one, over Stainmoor. At Bowes on or about 11 November, the Scots were turned back by the intervention of God and Saint Cuthbert. Supernatural events took place: 'Such a storm of snow and ice rose up that many of them died of cold and hunger'. Where before there had been no opposition to them, Saint Cuthbert had inspired the people of his county to rise against the invaders. An unspecified but large number of Durham men was reported by Scottish scouts to be marching against them, while the Scots themselves had fewer than one hundred horsemen and under three thousand infantry. This was nevertheless a powerful force; its size may explain the desertion of many Englishmen which even the English chronicler cannot disguise. Despite these defections the Scots were dismayed: 'If men were lacking, the power of Saint Cuthbert was in no way diminished [and] the enemy's plan to enter his land was foiled'.

By now the momentum of the Scots was halted. The weather was increasingly severe, they were weighed down by their booty, and their rebuff by Saint Cuthbert would have convinced them that they could expect no more. Wallace himself could not remain absent from Scotland indefinitely. In his absence those elements in the country over which he had to maintain the control which Stirling had brought him could not be relied on to adhere to the cause of Balliol. The raid into England, if it had failed to capture a single town, had been successful in inflicting a memorable punishment on the English. The name of Wallace would not be readily forgotten. The Scots were bringing back a considerable booty with them as evidence of their weeks over the Border. As they returned home, the Scots still had time for a last orgy of destruction in the lower valley of the Tyne.

Wallace was back in Scotland towards the end of November. Guisborough relates that before the return over the Border, he gave to the contingent from Galloway their entitlement from the booty. The Gallovidians were not the easiest of allies for any Scottish leader, for they looked upon themselves as a separate entity. They had long enjoyed a reputation for cruelty, and it is certain that in 1297, as before, they were well to the forefront in the perpetration of the atrocities which occurred in the raid. For Wallace they would have been useful shock troops, brave if undisciplined, fearful to behold, utterly ruthless. It would be natural to see in them the thieves of the incident at Hexham priory. Wallace would not be unhappy to be rid of them once he had decided to return to Scotland.

The raid had achieved nothing in terms of practical or strategic value and may therefore be thought a luxury, an indulgence. Wallace himself would not, however, have seen it as such, for his aims were more immediate and limited. We cannot doubt that the raid was a popular move. Indeed, it was necessary to strengthen still further his hold over affairs. To those who, for him, counted, the people, the raid brought retribution upon the English and plunder. Although a longer absence from Scotland would have been dangerous for him, the name he had earned at Stirling was sufficient to allow of no opposition from within the country. When, therefore, he came back to Scotland he was able to assume the reins of government with no apparent difficulty.

By now, of course, he was deprived of the presence of Murray. If it made any difference to him, there is no record of it. His principal concern was to prepare for the onslaught which would come from Edward I. That and the continued government of Scotland would have taxed any man, of whatever origins. Wallace's relatively humble birth, never as lowly as the English portrayed it, was an obstacle to the cooperation of those who considered themselves his superiors. That obstacle, at least in theory, was removed by his knighting. That symbolic act took place at some time before 29 March 1298.[19] On that date he was at Torphichen in West Lothian where he issued the charter to Alexander Scryngeour to which reference has already been made. In it we find him referring to himself both as Knight and Guardian. Who bestowed the knighthood is not known; from a remark in an English chronicle it must, almost certainly, have been one of the premier earls. A case has been made for Bruce,[20] but definite proof is lacking. The knighthood moved Wallace several rungs up, as it were, on the social ladder. It afforded him of itself a certain authority, not least in his relationships with others.

More significant, although associated with the bestowing of knighthood, was Wallace's election to the Guardianship. The two may, indeed, have occurred in the course of the same ceremony; there is no record of the date of either. Wallace was sole Guardian, the choice of a special council of nobles and churchmen. His was a massive achievement. The English, in one of their political songs, poured scorn and hatred on what he had done: 'After this [Stirling] the leader of the plot calls together his party, knowing that our king would be gone over the sea; he made an order to ravage Northumberland . . . William Wallace is the leader of these savages . . . To increase the wickedness which they had hitherto perpetrated, these wicked men deliver Alnwick to the flames . . . Now the malignant people returns to Scotland; and the honour of knighthood is given to William; from a robber he becomes a knight, just as a swan is made out of a raven; an unworthy man takes the seat, when a worthy man is not by'.[21] If we may wonder whether Wallace did not need to wait upon Edward's departure for

France to strike at the English, we may also readily believe that what he had been given, he had earned by his own merit. The abuse of this and other songs is the clearest proof of his accomplishment. The fear in which the English held him was well deserved. To their credit, the Scots, with the knighthood and the election as Guardian, had seen in him something more than the scourge of the English. They had seen in him a man possessed of unique talents: a soldier and a statesman. If it was an uncommon combination, the task ahead was daunting.

It is likely that in the aftermath of his knighting Wallace was forced to leave the fine detail of government in the hands of those more experienced in this work than himself: the clerks, the bishops, those officials who had returned to their posts as Cressingham wrote of the distintegration of the English hold over Scotland. Wallace's strong hand was, however, seen in one crucial matter at least. On 20 August, 1297, William Fraser, bishop of St. Andrews and a former Guardian, died at Auteuil, near Paris. Fraser had played a leading role in the negotiations with France in 1295 and never saw Scotland again.[22] Wallace, devoted to the Church in Scotland and well aware of its role in the struggle against England, saw the necessity of replacing the patriot, Fraser, with a man of like persuasion. How the English saw the election of a successor to Fraser is obvious from their later charge that Wallace had compelled the installation of William Lamberton.[23] When the day came, as they hoped, that the English domination of Scotland was to be re-established, they would need reliable prelates sympathetic to the English cause to help maintain that domination. Lamberton was not one such, as his later career was to prove.[24] He was to suffer greatly, on the orders of Edward I, for his part in the rising of Bruce. Threatened, abused, imprisoned with his fellow bishop Wishart, always with the knowledge that the unstable English king was capable of having him executed, he was not deflected from his determination to see Scotland independent. This he lived to see, for it was not until 1328, the year of the Treaty of Edinburgh and its ratification at Northampton, that he died. It was on the instructions of Wallace, given while he was in England, that Lamberton was elected to the see of St. Andrews. It was not the least of his bequests to the future of Scotland.

For the foremost authority on the period, 'the three main achievements of Wallace's regime were the invasion of Northumbria, the filling of the vacant see of St. Andrews, and the successful revival of the idea of guardianship'.[25] The first may be seen as the natural expression of the drive of an outstanding soldier bent on revenge against an enemy as implacable and violent as himself. The second, if it reflects a political wisdom, no less demonstrates a grasp of reality; he saw, and acted upon, the necessity of keeping the Church in the hands of those whose dedication to the Scottish cause was unquestioned. The third required of him outstanding, even unique, qualities. He had to achieve and hold on to what was by no means open to him. If he had the support of the people, if the Church, practical as ever, recognised in him the saviour of its independence from English claims to superiority, the magnates would be sceptical if not cynical. They were as practical as the prelates. For the English, the magnates' loyalty to Edward I was liable to melt away 'as frost in May'.[26] With Edward they had at least the rapport of nobility, the common experience of upbringing and aspirations. With Wallace they could not pretend to that. For later generations their loyalty to him was as dubious as that to Edward. That may be too simple an explanation. Wallace would, however, be unable to take their support for granted. When he was brought to trial in 1305, he faced the charge, among others, that he had persuaded and urged the magnates and prelates to fight with Philip IV of France against the English. His methods of convincing the recalcitrant were often, as has been seen, based more on fear than on reason. There is more than one kind of patriotism; Wallace's was not necessarily that of the magnates. For them, more than for him, the ends, in the phrase, justified the means. Had he understood that, he might have survived. But he did not; it is unlikely that he could have done. He must have been conscious of the possibility of defection, even if he did not anticipate treachery. The problem of the magnates must have occupied a large part of his thinking as, in the first half of 1298, he looked to the south. Edward I had returned to England from Flanders on 14 March. The king, no less singleminded than Wallace himself, now devoted all his energies to the problem of Scotland and the defeat of Wallace. He was an angry man, one who considered himself betrayed. Nothing was to be allowed to interfere with his obsession.

NOTES

1. See, for example, Barrow: *Robert Bruce*, 126; Prestwich, 48.

2. Most notably, of course, Barron.

3. The nature of the wound or the circumstances in which he received it are not recorded. Barron, chap. 7, deals with the former belief that he had, in fact, been killed in the battle.

4. It is surely based on nothing other than the appearance of his name, with that of Wallace, on such documents as have survived.

5. *Cal. Docs. Scot.*, iv, 1835.

6. Guisborough, 271-2, for Robert de Ros. Scrymgeour was executed at Newcastle on the orders of Edward I on 4 August 1306 as an adherent of Robert I.

7. It is impossible to say how much energy Wallace devoted to the capture of such castles. He does not appear, as far as we know, to have undertaken the building of the necessary engines or to have enlisted in his service engineers who might be capable of educating him. It was not, of course, an art in which the Scots in general seem to have been interested at this period.

8. The English were as enthusiastic as the Scots in this regard, e.g. Guisborough, 307-8.

9. There are certain periods of Bruce's career which pose difficulties even for the most dedicated of his biographers. If Falkirk is perhaps the most obvious of these, his actions after Irvine remain unclear also. At what stage he became, as McNair Scott says (53), once more the 'leader of the resistance in the south west' is open to question. Not even Barrow, who describes Bruce (*Robert Bruce*, 119) as 'inept' at Irvine explains how he might have achieved the necessary ability, after Irvine, to rank high in the immediate aftermath. It is, of course, true that as a major contender for the throne he could never be ignored.

10. See note 8 above for reference.

11. The comparison between Irvine and Stirling must, equally, have been obvious to contemporaries.

12. Barrow: *Robert Bruce*, 127.

13. Dickinson, Donaldson, Milne (eds.): *A Source Book of Scottish History*, I, 1985, 136-7.

14. Guisborough, 306.

15. Kightly, 168, treats briefly the possible reasons for the raid into England.

16. Guisborough, 303-7 and Lanercost, 190-1 should be consulted for the events.

17. Barrow: *Robert Bruce*, 131.

18. Guisborough,

19. The earliest use of the title.

20. McNair Scott, 241.

21. Wright: *Political Songs*, 172–173.

22. On the career of Fraser, see Barrow: *Robert Bruce, passim,* and the same author's *Kingdom of the Scots*, 236-8 and 246.

23. Palgrave, *Documents and Records*, 332, 339.

24. His relationship with Wallace, like that of Wishart with Wallace, was a strange one. Although he did not cease while in France to exhort Wallace to continue the fight against Edward, he did not himself find it a problem to collaborate with the English king in 1305.

25. Barrow; *Robert Bruce*, 130.

26. Wright: *Political Songs*, 214.

CHAPTER 6

The Time of Despair, 1298

The defeat at Stirling had, as no one could have anticipated, eased Edward's position at home. The slaughter of the English army, the undignified escape of Surrey, the treatment of the body of the dead Cressingham, these were insults not to be borne. There is no evidence that the English as a whole had formed as a result of Stirling a more favourable opinion of the Scots ability in war. Undoubtedly, however, there was a spirit of revenge in the air. Whatever problems Edward had faced before his departure for the Continent, he returned to a country united against the Scots in general and against Wallace in particular as it had never been. The threat of civil war disappeared.[1] The discontent of the nobles, led by the earls of Norfolk and Hereford, had already been alleviated in Edward's absence when Prince Edward, acting as regent, had become reconciled with the earls on 10 October of the previous year. From Ghent Edward himself had accepted his son's action, and he declared himself ready to give his assent to undertakings given in his name by the prince. These he would confirm at a parliament called for York at Whitsuntide. The clergy, no less affected by the need for reconciliation, produced subsidies for the forthcoming campaign from the provinces of York and Canterbury. Mindful as the clergy were of the opportunities which the subjugation of Scotland offered, such subsidies, involving as they did the protection of England, were to be distinguished from others intended for use in foreign adventures. The chronicles and songs of the period sustained the vilification of Wallace. Edward knew well how to exploit the goodwill of his subjects.

His army was ordered to muster at Roxburgh for Wednesday 25 June.[2] He himself, in his determination to avenge Stirling, was at pains not to neglect any potential source of support. Before going to York for the parliament summoned for Whitsuntide, he had toured a number of shrines in the south of his kingdom, notably that at Walsingham, to seek inspiration and guidance. But it was upon the northern saints, over whose jurisdiction Wallace had ranged the previous winter, that he concentrated his attention. He first went as a supplicant to the shrine of John of Beverley and bore away with him the saint's banner as insurance against defeat in the campaign.[3]

It was an action sure to win favour with his army, for Edward was aware of the propaganda value of what he did. John, bishop of Hexham from 687 and then of York from 705, enjoyed great and deserved popularity with the English. His power was well attested. Even after the translation of his remains from their original resting-place to the grander location of York on 25 October 1037, his shrine at Beverley continued to be a centre of pilgrimage. It was assured of his protection against enemies of whatever kind. In 1069, while William I was crushing the last of rebellion in the north of England, Beverley was saved from destruction by the intervention of the saint. John was especially potent in battle; his name had been on the lips of the English in the savage wars of the Scottish border for centuries. The passage of time did not detract from his authority or his fame. Henry V, the equal of Edward I as a soldier, ascribed the victory of Agincourt to John.

Edward's visit to Beverley has been seen[4] as a deliberate imitation of that undertaken by Athelstan, king of the English, who at Brunanburh in 937 defeated the alliance of Constantine, king of Alba, Owan, king of Strathclyde, and Guthfrithson, leader of the Danes of Dublin. Constantine lost his eldest son in the battle, and no fewer than five minor kings and five earls are said to have died with him. Athelstan, in traditional fashion, went on to ravage Scotland. Edward, a propagandist of no little skill if no exceptional honesty, would be content to let the parallel between himself and his successful predecessor be remarked among those he commanded.

To the banner of one saint he next took the precaution of adding another, that of Cuthbert of Durham, whose reputation as defender of the English, miracle worker, and inveterate foe of the Scots outstripped even that of John of Beverley. Less than a year before Edward's appeal to him Cuthbert had given evidence of his aweful power over the affairs of men. It was then that he had turned back Wallace and his army from the borders of Durham. Not only had the saint aroused in the men of the county the will to challenge the invincible Scots, he had called up a winter storm of such ferocity that Scots died where they stood and Wallace was forced to abandon his plans.[5]

Far from being the routine behaviour of a superstitious man, Edward's public veneration of the northern saints and his enlisting of their aid was part of the policy, initiated upon his return from Flanders, of maintaining that feverish hatred of Wallace which sprang from the latter's achievements. Not until the murder of Comyn in February 1306 would Edward again be able to rouse his people to such a pitch of patriotic fervour. Under his direction the campaign of 1298 was assuming the nature of a holy war. Wallace had challenged the king's supremacy and must be made to pay.

The English might continue to grumble at the increasingly heavy taxes they were made to pay to subsidise the war in Scotland,[6] the nobility might still regard their king with some suspicion, but Edward rode to battle in the well-founded belief that the country was with him. For Wallace there was no such certainty. In a song of the period,[7] written shortly after Falkirk, the mood of the English is unequivocal. The English, as might be expected, are conquerors, compared to angels, provoked into righteous retaliation by the perfidy of their enemies. Edward's wrath, great though it is, is just. He is the chosen of God, from whom he derives the strength to chastise the Scots, as he had already chastised the Welsh and the French. Wallace is not spared. He is 'a robber', 'unworthy', 'scarcely better than a mouse'. His cruelty and viciousness in the north of England are recorded. Those he leads are 'filthy', 'swine', 'malignant', 'savages', 'murderers'. They cannot expect to escape punishment for that treachery which alone explains the success they have had. 'Let them perish utterly both fathers and sons', the song calls. This, although common some thirty years later,[8] is far beyond the ritual exchange of insults in which both sides had always indulged. Thus, with the absolute certainty that the saints watched over his venture, knowing that his people, however much they might complain, were united behind him in his mission to deal with Wallace, Edward made his way into Scotland by way of Newcastle and Alnwick, where he rested briefly before proceeding to Roxburgh. There he arrived in early July.

That part of the Falkirk campaign which began with the departure of the English army from Roxburgh has, perhaps not surprisingly in view of the importance attached to the battle itself, received less attention that it deserves. This neglect of a significant phase of the campaign has damaged Wallace's reputation, unjustly. Once Edward set out from Roxburgh a pattern developed, soon to become familiar and destructive of the morale of successive English armies in Scotland. As a matter of policy, Edward devastated the land over which he passed. The consequences of such a policy appear to have escaped as seasoned a soldier as he was. It is, of course, possible that he was relying for the provisioning of his troops on the grain ships which were then making their way up the east coast. But there is some evidence that, although he meant to settle with Wallace, he was also intent on a punitive expedition;[9] he did not eschew destruction for its own sake and as a warning to the Scots. They, meanwhile, had retired before him, in the belief that the situation was to their advantage. The country south of the Forth was empty of inhabitants; Edward was short of intelligence, his men of sustenance.[10] Wallace knew very well the value of such a withdrawal; it formed an integral part of his strategy. Such a technique was not the creation of Robert I, although his successful

C: Carlisle L: Lochmaben N: Newcastle R: Roxburgh
E: Edinburgh L: Linlithgow F: Falkirk S: Stirling P: Perth
St A: St Andrews LA: Lauder D: Dalhousie T: Temple Liston

Map 2. The Falkirk Campaign, 1298. The arrows indicate Edward's advance: at Falkirk 22 July. The solid line indicates Edward's withdrawal: at Carlisle 9 September.

employment of it against the armies of Edward II has somewhat obscured the fact. There is a parallel here with Edward II's invasion of 1322; so lacking were the English then in food that they are reported to have found in the whole of Lothian only one cow. At that, the earl of Surrey, son of Wallace's old enemy, commented that he had never seen dearer beef.[11] His father, riding with Edward I and in similar straits, would have understood the sentiment. How close Wallace came to victory over Edward without a fight will emerge. It is too often forgotten that only with hindsight do the events of July 1298 assume their familiar shape. Wallace was content to draw the English on, and the wisdom of that tactic was to become apparent.

Although we lack precise evidence as to his movements at the time of the English advance, we may reasonably make certain basic assumptions. There must have been a strong temptation to meet the English early rather than later; there always was. Wallace cannot have taken the decision to avoid confrontation with the English in the south-east without great thought. Edward had chosen to lead his army through an area which was and would remain a fighting-ground. While it is true that it was an area in which the Scots were unsuccessful in military terms, they did not hesitate to fight there. Dunbar had been but one of a series of defeats suffered by the Scots in this part of the country. Pinkie, and, again, Dunbar lay in the future. The route which Edward followed, through Lauderdale and thus to the outskirts of Edinburgh which he reached on 11 July, was that favoured by English armies invading from the east. It was therefore a natural focal point for an assault upon the invader. News of his ravaging of the land would reach Wallace. It would rouse the anger of his men. It is not unlikely that Edward intended this.

Yet Wallace was not tempted. He did not deviate from his plan. He waited, as Robert I would wait in other campaigns. Wallace's decision to stand on the defensive, to allow for the wasting of the English army, had been taken well in advance of the invasion. He must have known that an opportunity to attack was possible. In the kind of war in which he believed, intelligence had a great role. Barrow has shown [12] how in this campaign he used contingents from the Lowlands; among these were men who came from the very area through which Edward was passing. From them would come the information he required. Nor would he be free of pressure from the nobles. Dunbar had taught them nothing; their inclination, like that of their English counterparts at Falkirk, was still to go on the offensive. Somehow, he had convinced them of the need for that restraint which not even harsh experience had shown them to be necessary. Wallace's own following, as will shortly be argued, was not inconsiderable. He may have used the threat of deploying it independently to force the nobles into agreement. It is equally possible, however, that he was forced to bargain with the nobles in order to secure their compliance. Their role, and, interestingly, that of the English nobles in the forthcoming battle indicates that the relationship between leader and led was neither an easy one nor strong even in the heat of events.

The price of that restraint which Wallace urged on his noble allies was to prove a serious one. Because he fought at Falkirk it has always been assumed that he intended from the beginning to give battle to Edward. Wallace's own inclination, however, was the quick strike and retreat, the mounted attack and withdrawal before a counter-attack could be made. Even Stirling does not contradict this; it proves rather that he was adept at seizing the God-given moment. Wallace's great achievement in keeping a Scottish army in existence and, without committing it, almost bringing Edward's plans to frustration, has not been sufficiently recognised. No one has explained how Scotland was to be defended without an army; we cannot be sure that Wallace saw the existence of the army he raised solely in terms of pitched battles. The disaster at Falkirk—for such it was and not just in terms of numbers killed—has proved too tempting for historians. It fits too well into the theory that, there, Wallace's period of supremacy was tidily if bloodily ended. What must be said is that no Scottish leader at this time would have scorned battle with the English, not least because of the practical difficulties of keeping an army unemployed in the field. Each would certainly have fought and, equally certainly, under more difficult conditions than those which Wallace provided for the Scots on 22 July.

The English advance was proving something of a disaster. If Edward's army was formidable in appearance and size, it was suffering both the consequences of a Scottish policy of scorched earth and the failure to maintain its own supplies. The most authoritative treatment gives Edward some two thousand horse and an infantry force in the region of twelve thousand.[13] The cavalry were a committed unit, half provided by those same earls who had brought the country not long before to the verge of civil war, the rest recruited by commissioners of array. Of the infantry, the greater part did not share the patriotism of the earls or the mercenary devotion of the other horse, for they were either Irish or Welsh and would soon show themselves unreliable. When, on 20 July, the army reached Temple Liston, Edward was forced to order the plunder of nearby Kirkliston, which belonged to bishop Lamberton, in the hope of relieving the hunger of his soldiers. It was no more than a temporary expedient. The few transport ships which made their way to Leith brought wine, not corn.[14]

While Edward was at Temple Liston, a revealing incident occurred.[15] He dispatched Antony Bek, bishop of Durham, to seize certain castles held by the Scots. Bek's men had no food other than the peas and beans which they lifted from the fields. With such a weak force and without siege engines Bek could see no hope of carrying out his instructions. He sent to Edward for new instructions. Edward's reply was indicative of his state of mind; to Bek's messenger he said: 'Go back and tell the bishop that as bishop he is a man of Christian piety, but Christian piety has no place in what he is doing now'. To the messenger himself, Sir John FitzMarmaduke, Edward addressed these still more chilling words: 'And as for you, you are a bloodthirsty man. I have often had to rebuke you for being too cruel. But now be off, use all your cruelty, and instead of rebuking you I shall praise you. Take care you don't see me until all three castles are burnt'. It was as if Edward regarded the Scots as being fit only for the harshest of treatment even at this early stage. FitzMarmaduke carried Edward's answer to Bek. In fear of their king and with the lucky arrival of food ships to encourage them, Bek's troops dealt speedily with the castles.

The success of Bek's men was not enough to raise the morale of the English army for long. Food was still short. Many of the Welsh infantry were literally dying of hunger. Edward now committed one of those errors which so damage his reputation as a soldier. He ordered that the Welsh should be given wine. This, far from solving the problem, inflamed them. Drunk, they fought with the English and a number of priests were killed. Edward could not prevent his knights from attacking the Welsh. Of the latter, some eighty were killed and the rest put to flight. The Welsh spent the night apart from the rest of the army, threatening to change sides. Strangely, Edward claimed to be indifferent. For him the Welsh were still enemies, it seemed; let them join the Scots. 'With God's help', he said, 'we shall then defeat the whole lot of them in one go.' No doubt this was bravado. Nevertheless, for the great general he was held to be, Edward, on this campaign, appears vulnerable and inept. Whatever misfortunes attended the passage of the supply ships, he had relied too heavily on this source of provisions. He miscalculated the mood of the Welsh and neglected the elementary task of ensuring their loyalty. If it is true that he learned from this campaign and was never again to repeat the mistakes he committed there, it is also true that he was only rescued from his own blundering by outside intervention.

That intervention came on 21 July.[16] So desperate was the English position that Edward had decided to retire upon Edinburgh as a preliminary to abandoning the invasion. What happened is told in detail in Guisborough, our most complete source.[17] It is ironic that it was two Scottish earls, Patrick of Dunbar and Gilbert de Umfraville of Angus, who brought to Edward the opportunity to redeem his reputation. Both had remained faithful to Edward, but the modern mind would find it less than easy to understand that allegiance. With them they had a scout or spy, it is not clear precisely which, who lifted Edward's heart with these words: 'My lord king, the Scots army and all your enemies are no more than eighteen miles from here, just outside Falkirk . . . . They have heard that you intend to retreat to Edinburgh, and they mean to follow you and attack your camp tomorrow night, or at least to fall on your rearguard and plunder your vanguard'. The significance of this description of Wallace's intention, although taken from the account most often used by historians of the period, is overlooked. It tells us clearly that Wallace did not intend the pitched battle which followed but aimed to use the English retreat in the most obvious way, the way which, in other circumstances, Wallace, a master of improvisation, would have chosen.

But he was to be denied the fulfilment of his plan. He was not given the time to make the sortie from what we must see as a fortified camp at Falkirk. He had pulled the English forward to the point where, weakened and in retreat, they would offer an easy target for one of those mounted assaults at which he was adept. Edward was saved by the two Scottish earls. He did not hesitate. His words tell of his relief: 'May God be praised, for He has solved all my problems. The Scots will have no need to follow me, for I will march to meet them at once'. Telling his troops to arm themselves, but without, it seems, informing them of their destination, he led them in the direction of Falkirk. That night the English host camped on the Burgh Muir, to the east of Linlithgow.[18] Edward clearly still expected just such an attack as he had been warned of by the Scottish earls; his men were to rest with their horses beside them.[19]

During the night Edward was slightly injured when his own horse trod on him. The news of the accident was enough to panic his army which feared both betrayal and an attack by the enemy. Their reaction was so extreme as to suggest that had Wallace been able to carry out his first intention, he would have had little difficulty in inflicting severe damage on the English. Edward, however, despite the pain from his ribs, dealt more successfully with the panic than he had with the problem of the Welsh. At dawn the English marched through Linlithgow. They soon came in sight of the enemy; on the top of a hill they saw many spearmen. At this the English moved forward in the belief that what they had seen was the main Scottish army. The spearmen, however, retreated and were lost to sight.

This incident has not been considered worthy of much attention. Yet it may be of consequence to an understanding of the battle of Falkirk. What was this body of spearman? It was large enough to cause apprehension among the English who took it for the Scottish army. It could have been a late addition to Wallace's forces; if so, such an arrival would in all probability have been noted in accounts of the battle. In the absence of proof, it is possible to advance a tentative theory: that Wallace, in keeping with his intention, as expressed in Guisborough, of attacking the English while they were in retreat, had begun to move away from Falkirk with that in mind. The spearmen, therefore, would be a contingent sent from the fortified site or camp as part of Wallace's plan. This would be consistent with the argument that he was, as at Stirling, intent on improvisation rather than on a setpiece battle. The spearmen, on seeing the English army, would therefore retire on the main Scottish army, bringing with them the unwelcome news of Edward's approach. Edward, quite literally, had, thanks to the report he had received, stolen a march on Wallace. The latter was forced to abandon his original intention. His army was forced to fight on terms which he had not chosen. That it fought so well tells us that it had been trained with the utmost efficiency.

Wallace's army on the feast of Saint Mary Magdalene, Tuesday 22 July, was the product of two basic determinants. It was predominantly composed of infantry. Scotland was too poor to be able to afford the maintenance of a large force of heavy armoured cavalry on the English model. Such few heavy cavalry as were present were in the gift of the nobles. We shall return in due course to the vexed question of the role of the nobles and their cavalry. If Wallace had always relied after Lanark on mobility to create the maximum effect, his men's mounts must have been light, unarmoured, their function the ancient one of transport to the site of whatever action he intended. At Falkirk, given the circumstances in which he was now to fight, these skirmishers – they cannot properly be called cavalry – would be dismounted and integrated into the mass of the infantry. It was upon the infantry that the outcome of the battle would depend.

After his raid into England, Wallace had begun the long process of creating a standing army. To do so, he used the power of his personality, the requirement that every man between the age of sixteen and sixty serve in arms to defend his country, and that weapon to which he never scrupled to have recourse, fear. Once Guardian, he had the further advantage of authority. The numbers who accepted the call to arms cannot have been great but their lack of experience, their indiscipline, and the natural fear of the conscripted soldier cannot have made Wallace's task other than difficult. His was, it must not be forgotten, the role of a commander without professional training. No doubt he could use the services of willing officers, men who had seen service in the earlier part of the war. The question of whether these officers included a contribution from the nobles must remain unanswered. If, as Barrow says,[20] the earls of Atholl, Menteith, Buchan, Lennox, and Carrick were among the contributors to the Scottish army, it is a far step from that to assigning them and their like the positive role of training the army. Responsibility for the training was Wallace's, as was the burden of defeat.

He had prepared the Scots, in a relatively short space of time, not only for the tactics at which he himself was so adept, but for exactly the test which now faced them. That is, the army was to stand on the defensive to receive the principal English weapon, the heavy cavalry. His dispositions are well recorded in the account found in Guisborough. Wallace had divided the infantry into four schiltroms, the first known mention of what became a standard feature of the war with England but so obvious a tactic as certainly to be well-established. Each of the four, Guisborough tells us, 'was made up, wholly of spearmen, standing shoulder to shoulder in deep ranks and facing towards the circumference of the circle, with their spears slanting outwards at an oblique angle'.[21] The hedgehog-like appearance of the schiltroms would be frightening, as it was intended to be. The schiltrom could be switched from the defensive to the offensive, as Robert I was able to do at Bannockburn. The twelve-inch, iron-tipped spears of the infantry were a powerful deterrent to the cavalry and at Falkirk, as again at Bannockburn, inflicted severe injury on the horses themselves. If, as almost happened, the English cavalry charges were held, the infantry would be converted into an advancing force whose weaponry, once its momentum had gathered, would be irresistible.

The infantry's defensive position had been further strengthened by a fence of stakes. Each of the four schiltroms was surrounded by this enclosure, the stakes, linked by ropes, pointing towards the English. If these enclosures baulked the cavalry, they would then be thrown aside to allow the infantry to proceed to the second stage, the attack. We do not know how many men stood on this day in each of the schiltroms. As the Scottish army is unlikely to have exceeded that of the English, each of the schiltroms would scarcely have contained more than two thousand men. Wallace had with him a small body of archers, men from the Forest of Selkirk. Archery was not a branch of warfare in which the Scots ever excelled. It does the men of Selkirk no disservice to say that their role at Falkirk, although a most honourable one, could never be as significant as that of Edward's bowmen. These, Welshmen armed with the longbow and Genoese mercenaries using the crossbow, could only be effectively countered by cavalry. We shall see how the precaution which Wallace had taken to nullify the menace of Edward's bowmen was thwarted.

Wallace's fortified camp, now a battle formation, was well sited for its new purpose. Its rear was protected by Callendar Wood. In front was the Westquarter Burn. The Scottish position on the south-east side of a hill near Falkirk was rendered stronger still by a boggy loch between it and the advancing English.[22]Wallace's choice of site has been criticised.[23] If it was not ideal, and inferior to that selected at Stirling, it proved almost as successful as on the earlier occasion. We must assume from what we know of Wallace that had he meant to fight at this point in the campaign, he would have arranged matters differently.

When the English saw Wallace's dispositions, the more sensible among them must have appreciated its strength. In Guisborough we read that Edward himself was against an immediate assault.[24] Conscious as he was that his men had not eaten for some twenty-four hours, he proposed a halt. It is impossible to believe that he was not affected at least as much by what awaited him. His opinion was not shared by his subordinates. Edward, surprisingly, could not restrain them. The earls of Norfolk, Hereford, and Lincoln among others refused to heed their king. Ignorant of the water obstacle which lay between them and the Scots, the English vanguard moved forward but were forced to swing west round the bog.[25] They must have presented an attractive target to the Scottish archers stationed between the schiltroms. Since there is no mention of the archers at this juncture, the opportunity does not appear to have been taken. On the opposite flank the knights were as enthusiastic as the vanguard. The flavour of their mettle emerges from the words of Ralph Bassett to their nominal commander, bishop Bek. The bishop, trying to ensure some discipline, was roundly told to mind his own business and to repeat the mass he had said before the battle.

The obstacle of the bog safely negotiated, the cavalry attacked the schiltroms. At the first contact the Scottish horse fled. The inevitable charge of treachery followed in Scottish accounts.[26] Whatever the motives of the cavalry, their flight was a disaster for Wallace. It was bad enough that they had not struck a blow. Worse, their absence was to allow free rein to the English archers. At Bannockburn Robert I kept in reserve a cavalry force of some five hundred under the command of the marshall of Scotland, Sir Robert Keith. Its task was to interrupt the work of the English archers. In the event Keith did more; he broke the lines of archers and they took to their heels. Their loss to Edward II was one of the turning points of Bannockburn. The presence of the future king of Scots at Falkirk is problematical.[27] He cannot have been ignorant, however, of its various phases. If Bruce learned much from Wallace, the use of horse against bowmen was one factor marked in his mind after Falkirk.

With the Scots cavalry gone, the schiltroms were alone. Sir John Stewart, brother of the Stewart, was killed along with his bowmen by the horse who were nevertheless still thwarted by the continued and heroic resistance of the schiltroms. Their weapons wrought much havoc on the

English mounts.[28] They could offer no such resistance to the English archers. Edward called back the cavalry. The Scots cannot have been ignorant of what was to come. It is easy to imagine their despair as they stood, impotent, to await the arrows. That they did not break argues well for the discipline which Wallace had instilled in them. They died in large numbers. One English chronicler celebrated the slaughter: 'They fell like blossoms in an orchard when the fruit has ripened'.[29] He goes on to relate that their 'bodies covered the ground as thickly as snow in winter'. These images, while hardly original, convey the horror of the battle as it was now.

When the archers and the slingers had done their work, Edward sent the knights against the thinning, demoralised ranks of the schiltroms. Some of the infantry escaped the arrows and lances only to perish by drowning in the bog below their position. The numbers of Scots who had died on this long day which culminated in a massacre cannot be given with any hope of accuracy. The majority were of the common people who had been Wallace's strength from the beginning. One would not expect their names to be recorded.[30] If unknown, their courage mocked the conduct of their betters. Not all of the latter had betrayed them. The Stewart's brother, John, met the same fate as his men. Fordun, who found an explanation of the Scottish defeat in the flight of the nobles, especially John Comyn the younger, tells us that Macduff of Fife was killed at Falkirk.[31] Guisborough relates that although the majority of the Scottish knights fled, a handful fought with the schiltroms.

Of the Scottish lords it is Robert Bruce, earl of Carrick and future king, whose role in respect of Falkirk is the most puzzling. He did not escape the censure of Scottish chroniclers. If their view that he led an English troop against the Scottish rear is dismissed as 'pure fiction' by one recent writer,[32] Bruce's most respected biographer twice admits to doubts about Bruce's part, even his presence at Falkirk.[33] Barron, who in an impassioned chapter defends Bruce against the charge that he was implicated in the death of Wallace,[34] does not place Bruce at the battle.[35] Like another recent biographer of Bruce,[36] he has him working for the Scottish cause in the south-west at the time of Falkirk. If the truth is that we do not know if Bruce was at Falkirk, we can venture that it is unlikely. He was too important a figure not to be mentioned as present if he was there. His activity elsewhere is clear. As with John Comyn, his adversary, his motives elude us. His role in the war since its start suggests equivocation. At the time of Falkirk his support of the Scottish cause did not, it would seem, include subordination to Wallace. Bruce, as always and again like Comyn, had his own plans and his own ambitions. Treachery, like patriotism, means different things to different men.

In an English chronicle,[37] Wallace is pictured uttering a memorable phrase to his army. Rendered into modern English from the original Scots, it reads: 'I have brought you into the ring: now see if you can dance'. The phrase may not, as has been suggested, be Wallace's own.[38] It hints at a despair which is not found elsewhere in his, admittedly few, recorded statements. It may be more realistic to interpret the sentiment as a recognition that he had done his best and that events must take their course. This would be more appropriate if, as has been argued, it was not his intention to fight at Falkirk. Once battle was joined, however, his ability to inspire as well as to prepare his army was demonstrated. His mistake was to rely on the support of the cavalry over whom he had not assumed control. Why he did not do so can best be explained by his unwillingness to alienate the nobles. He had not, of course, had experience of handling a force of heavy horse, but we know of no attempt by him to find a commander of horse sympathetic to his ends. Had he done so, the cavalry would, it may be argued, have been used as it was at Bannockburn. What the outcome of Falkirk would then have been must remain an intriguing mystery. He left the cavalry in the control of the lords, perhaps as part of that bargain by which they continued to tolerate, if not support, his tactics of withdrawal. Without that control and the opportunity for glory which, before the battle, it offered, they would have been less willing to continue with his army. Their defection at Falkirk was crucial, but it would be unreasonable to blame Wallace for failing to anticipate and then to prevent it. With that defection the English archers were free. Their work began the slaughter of Falkirk, a battle which brought to an end a campaign by Wallace which was a model for its time and a study for another, more celebrated Scot.

NOTES

1. Powicke, 687; Salzman, 141; McNair Scott, 49.
2. Palgrave: *Parl. Writs*, i. 312-316.
3. Guisborough, 324; *Cal. Docs. Scot.*, ii, 1177.
4. Barrow: *Robert Bruce*, 140.
5. Wallace himself may not have found the saint's intervention unwelcome. His army must by this time have been in some disarray. The problems of carrying back to Scotland the booty which had been taken, the lack of control over the men of Galloway, and the knowledge that he was needed back in Scotland would have been troubling him.
6. The mood is reflected most clearly in Wright: *Political Songs, passim*.
7. Wright: *Political Songs*, 160-180, *passim*.

8. On the effects of the war upon English society and on the increasing bitterness against the Scots which the war produced, see Prestwich, 72-77. A more detailed if specialised discussion of the effects of the war is to be found in Scammell: 'Robert I and the North of England', *E.H.R.*, lxxiii, 385-403.

9. Guisborough, 324-5.

10. *Ibid.*

11. Barbour: *Bruce*, 330.

12. 'Lothian in the First War of Independence', *S.H.R.*, Oct. 1976, 151-171.

13. Barrow: *Robert Bruce*, 139.

14. Guisborough, 325.

15. Guisborough, 324-5.

16. *Ibid.*

17. *Ibid.*

18. Guisborough, 326.

19. *Ibid.*

20. *Robert Bruce*, 143n.

21. Guisborough, 327.

22. *Ibid.*

23. Salzman, 143, says: 'Wallace had not selected his position with any great skill'. Kightly, 178, writes that his position was 'nothing like so strong as the one he had occupied at Stirling'. Barron, 78, states that the Scots prepared to meet the English 'in a situation which had few natural advantages and, from which, in the event of misfortune, there was not easy means of escape'. Barrow: *Robert Bruce*, 143, while arguing that the position was inferior to that at Stirling, accepts that 'it was not badly chosen for the kind of battle he wished to fight'. Dickinson, 159, and McNair Scott share this view, although suggesting that Wallace should not have fought at all.

24. Guisborough, 327.

25. *Ibid.*

26. Fordun, i, 330. Barrow: *Robert Bruce*, 144 acquits them of the charge of treachery and suggests that they were overcome by panic. He equates their conduct at Falkirk with their behaviour at Dunbar and Irvine. It might be thought that a succession of such failures was in itself a form of treachery, the more so when in the case of Falkirk their role was crucial; they surely betrayed Wallace himself, if not the army, by their flight.

27. Neither McNair Scott nor Barrow can place Bruce at Falkirk on the Scottish side. Both evade the issue by concentrating on his activity after the battle. McNair Scott, 52; Barrow: *Robert Bruce*, 145. If, as Barrow says (*Robert Bruce*, 144), Fordun, for example, had to 'show the Comyns in as black a light as possible', Fordun would surely have found some way of proving Bruce's conduct to be the opposite. The silence on Bruce's presence, let alone on a heroic role, would seem to argue that he was not on the Scottish side.

28. *Cal. Docs. Scot.*, ii, 1007, 1011.

29. Rishanger.

30. Barrow: 'Lothian in the First War of Independence' should be consulted for some names.

31. Fordun, i, 330.

32. Kightly, 180. He does, however, add: 'if present at all, he was fighting on the Scots side'.

33. Barrow: *Robert Bruce*, 145. See also n. 27 above.

34. Barron, Chap. 15.

35. Barron, 77, 78, 181.
36. McNair Scott. 50.
37. Rishanger, 187.
38. Salzman, 143.

CHAPTER 7

The Time of Sacrifice, 1298–1303

Modern commentators are agreed that Wallace's resignation of the Guardianship was the direct and inevitable consequence of the defeat at Falkirk.[1] His reputation and therefore his hold on the office, it is argued, depended upon continued military success. Denied that, and lacking as he did the advantage of hereditary position or authority on which to fall back, he would thus have had no alternative to resignation. Whether he gave up his office willingly or otherwise is not known, but it is generally accepted that the opposition of the magnates to him and to what he represented contributed in some measure to his withdrawal from the leadership of the resistance to Edward. There is, undoubtedly, a certain appealing neatness about the sequence of defeat and resignation. It allows for the supremacy of Wallace to be seen as an episode, glorious in itself, but still an episode.

Wallace's resignation, however, and the reasons for it, cannot be so easily dismissed. Scottish popular tradition has long judged him with sympathy. The belief persisted that he was so outraged by the conduct of the Scottish lords at Falkirk that he no longer wished to associate with them and so decided upon resignation. We find this attitude in Fordun: 'But after the aforesaid victory, which was vouchsafed for the enemy through the treachery of Scots, the aforesaid William Wallace, perceiving by these and other strong proofs, the glaring wickedness of the Comyns and their abettors, chose rather to serve with the crowd, than to be set over them, to their ruin, and the grievous wasting of the people. So, not long after the battle, at the water of Forth, he, of his own accord, resigned the office and charge which he held, of guardian'.[2]

It would appear, at first glance, that Fordun accepts the link between Falkirk and Wallace's resignation, although emphasising the treachery of his allies at the battle as crucial. Betrayal by Bruce as well as by Comyn cannot be discounted,[3] but it is unlikely to have been the main or only explanation of Wallace's resignation. Fordun does after all mention other factors influencing Wallace. He tells us that Wallace preferred to return to his roots, to his own people, rather than to continue at their head, to their ultimate detriment. We need not question that he did indeed wish to make such a return. To do so was not to admit to failure but to act in a realistic and responsible manner. His departure from the field of Falkirk illustrates this clearly. To the English, not unnaturally, he had fled the battle. Celebrating the carnage among the Scots, the English sang of Wallace: 'Scared by the fear of punishment, the tyrant turns his back, whom the short jacket once pleased: faithless in the day of battle he flies like a truant . . . Wallace, thy reputation as a soldier is lost, since thou didst not defend thy people with the sword, it is just that thou shouldst now be deprived of thy dominion'.[4]

This judgment is, of course, preposterous. Wallace's courage was never at issue; it was not the least of his attributes, entirely to be expected of him. In this, if in no other way, he bears a strange resemblance to Edward II at Bannockburn. We read of that unhappy monarch bent on fighting to the death but advised to leave the field for reasons of state.[5] So it was with Wallace at the earlier battle. He could not permit himself the luxury of a death sword in hand; he was of value to his country and its cause only if he remained alive. He could no longer save the army once Edward had forced a breach in its ranks, but he could retire to prepare further his role in the defence of Scotland. Major rationalises his behaviour thus: 'There are those still living in our midst who will not suffer the word 'flight' to be used in reference to Wallace, and will only allow that he avoided a danger; for flight, they say, must ever bear an ugly meaning. But in this they err. To attack the attacker by waiting for him; to delay; yea, to fly – these too are branches of fortitude; for the greatest general that ever lived may fly but in a certain contingency is bound to fly. For better it is that he should be able to keep himself and his men in safety against a fitting moment than by their death bring ruin quick and complete upon his country. Wherefore Wallace was justified in seeking safety for his men in flight'.[6]

Like Pluscarden,[7] Major, further, has Wallace meet with Bruce after the battle and in a famous setpiece reply to the latter's accusation that he had acted above himself and his station. Wallace is made to speak in moving terms both of his reasons for resignation and of his confidence in the people whom Bruce so despises. If we accept that Wallace, as we are told in these and other sources, was intent upon severing his association with the lords and relying henceforth upon the people from whom he had sprung, we may be close to the real reason for his resignation of the office of Guard-ian.

That reason cannot be understood unless one widely held assumption is looked at: that Wallace had no alternative to resignation. Modern opinion, as has been seen, stresses the inevitability of resignation. It is, however, interesting, that early sources such as Fordun, together with tradition, imply that, for whatever reason, Wallace *decided* upon resignation; he had, that is, made a choice. We do not know when exactly he resigned; those who draw the connection between defeat and resignation do not offer a firm date for the latter.[8] It is possible, therefore, that Wallace pondered his decision for some time, perhaps over a period of weeks. He had learned patience as Guardian; the army which he marshalled, trained, and brought to Falkirk was the product of months of work as was the co-operation, however fragile in the event, which he had forged with the likes of Comyn and Bruce. He had become a wiser, if now a sadder, man. That being so, it is not unreasonable to suppose, lacking as we do any irrefutable proof to the contrary, that he must have debated the possibility that he could, despite Falkirk, retain power.

This is less of a fanciful suggestion than it may appear. There is no evidence that Wallace left the battle alone, quite the contrary, nor can it seriously be argued that his departure proved prejudicial among the people. Others, as we know, left either with him or about the same time.[9] It is probable that the Scottish lords, whose ranks had by no means been decimated, made their own way without Wallace, to avoid what they saw as the taint of association with him. But Fordun tells us that Wallace escaped 'to save himself and his',[10] a vague formula, it is true, open to more than one construction. Pluscarden, on the other hand, limits those who accompanied him to 'but few'.[11] Major writes of the 'surviving remnant of his army' which he took with him.[12] If we cannot be precise as to the numbers with him, Wallace had some kind of force with him and, despite the slaughter at Falkirk, it would be of some consequence. If we return, briefly, to Wallace's role in the battle, we may find some support for this theory. He would have had with him on the day a nucleus of adherents upon whom he had come to rely greatly, such as had been with him from the early days, men who formed – and this was not contrary to established practice – a bodyguard. They would, through their attachment to their leader, be tried and proven soldiers. And can we lightly dismiss the thought that Wallace had foreseen the need for some such group, a need demonstrated beyond argument by the defection of others?

Two other factors must be considered in this context. The first relates to the famous remark attributed to him as he addressed the Scottish army before Falkirk.[13] If there is any truth in it, it shows a man who believed that he had done the best he could for those under his command, and that now, with his preparations completed, he would put his talents to use wherever circumstances dicated. He would not have allocated himself a place in the schiltroms. It follows from this that, second, he would not have remained stationary, an obvious and attractive target to the enemy, as the battle progressed and the superiority of the English became evident. With his own group – his household troops, as it were – he would have moved about the field, to encourage, to support, to prompt. Not all of those with him can have been killed.

When at length he withdrew from the battle, he had about him, therefore, a force still capable of striking at the enemy. There is an account of a pursuit of Wallace by some of the English which seems to make this very point.[14] While this is romanticised by Major[15] in that Wallace himself turns upon the pursuers and kills one who has been unwise enough to outstrip his companions, the account does ring true. The departure of Wallace can hardly have gone unremarked by the English, and the subsequent pursuit could have involved a more general action than that reported, albeit a limited one quickly over. It is perhaps significant that Sir Brian le Jay, who with Sir John de Sawtry is the only English casualty of importance to be named by the chronicler,[16] is said to have been despatched by Scots when his horse plunged into a bog. The story has all the elements of a classic ambush with the foolhardy Englishman, and possibly others with him, lured to his death. Wallace was not a man to miss such an opportunity. The death of the master of the English Templars has the mark of Wallace.˙ It would have proved that he and his men, far from being demoralised by defeat and concerned only with saving their skins, were to be reckoned with. There is no further mention of pursuit at this time.

Events were to show that Wallace the popular hero survived the battle even if his position as Guardian was called into question. As was the case to the end of his life, he was able to attract followers; Falkirk was not enough to destroy the devotion he had inspired. Once, like other survivors, he had disappeared into 'the woods and castles'[17] north of Falkirk, he succeeded in moving quickly enough and with sufficient support to constitute a threat to the English as they advanced, tentatively and, it may be, reluctantly. The burning of Stirling and Perth to deny succour to the English has been attributed to him.[18] No one argues that Edward had won Scotland with his victory at Falkirk, but Professor Barrow has stated that the resistance to Edward was immediately taken over by the nobles.[19] But Wallace was still capable of playing a significant role after Falkirk. He still enjoyed the sympathy of the people on whom he would have drawn for reinforcements, and was as committed as ever to the cause which dominated his life. It may be suspected also that, as he had done before,[20] he dragooned the unwilling to join with him. By his presence he was menacing, and not only to the English.

Wallace was powerful enough to refuse to give up the office of Guardian. If this be doubted, one question must be faced: who was to replace him?

There were obvious candidates and, as time would prove, no shortage of them. Let it be remembered, however, that from the little we know, Wallace was not replaced at once. The defeat at Falkirk surely rendered that impossible. If Wallace had left the field for his own good reasons, others of note had either fled or beaten a tactical retreat. Survival was more urgent than discussion. Although we do not know when Wallace resigned, it would have required a formal meeting of the Scottish leadership for the decision to be taken. No such meeting would be possible without preparation; our sources indicate that the Scots leaders must have scattered after the battle.[21] Once they were reunited, hard bargaining must have been a feature of the meeting no less than recriminations, and Wallace would be in a position, if he so elected, to influence that bargaining and in no little measure. He would not have come alone, any more than would Bruce or Comyn, and his supporters would have watched over the negotiations, a reminder of what he represented. Nor would he have risked a further betrayal, the chance that he would fall a prey to his enemies in the Scottish camp. He cannot have been other than a potent figure at the time of his resignation.

That resignation, and his replacement in the Guardianship, has never been placed more accurately than within the period July to December 1298. Our deplorable lack of certainty on this subject allows it to be argued that negotiations over both were protracted. Wallace's resignation would therefore not have been immediate, and his role in this period would be a more important one than is usually conceded to him. He would want to ensure his own position but, more crucial to him, to ensure if possible a satisfactory outcome to the negotiations. If that is so, it is significant that those who accepted, even pressed for, his resignation, were unable even at a time of the gravest danger for Scotland to agree on one man to take his place.

Instead, two were appointed, a clear acknowledgement of the problem caused by Wallace's departure from the Guardianship. Robert Bruce and John Comyn the younger of Badenoch together filled the office held formerly by Wallace himself. It is of course indisputable that the office was never considered to be the province of any one man, nor had it been so in practice.[22] But Wallace had laid a quite unique claim to it, and after his departure no other individual emerged with the necessary authority, either personal or inherited, to stand in his place. The alliance between Bruce and Comyn has been hailed as evidence of Bruce's patriotism[23] in that he subordinated his claim to the throne of Scotland, and as proof that the Scots were determined on the survival of the principle of Guardianship.[24] A more detached view of the relationship might be that the Scots lords were again unwilling to put aside their self-interest in the cause of their country. Bruce would not entrust the office to Comyn who, for him, represented the Balliol faction, although Balliol was, legally, still king. Comyn, for his part, was equally suspicious; he was not prepared to concede that Bruce might be the better choice to lead the Scots in the struggle against Edward.

It does not require hindsight to believe that the alliance between Bruce and Comyn was an unlikely one and doomed not to last. In an incident to which we shall return, the two men were at blows in the course of a meeting at Peebles in August 1299. It was a sordid affair unrelated to the safety of Scotland but underlines the tension and mistrust between the Guardians. Bruce resigned possibly as early as November 1299 and certainly not later than May of the following year, when his place was taken by Ingram de Umfraville. The joint Guardianship of Bruce and Comyn, that is, lasted at most no more than eighteen months, and from its inception was ill-founded. Wallace could not have been unaware of this. He knew both men well, had striven during his tenure of the Guardianship to reconcile them, and had suffered from their selfishness. He was astute, as he must have been to hold together the disparate elements in Scotland in the months after he assumed the Guardianship. He was a man of great presence, with a partisan and hardened following, in numbers perhaps the equal of those following either Bruce or Comyn. Given all this, is it not possible that he could – by recourse to a simple expedient – have remained either as sole Guardian or as one of a number of Guardians, and therefore able to influence if not dictate policy and events?

Wallace need have done no more than enter into a pact with Bruce or, perhaps more plausible because of their common allegiance to Balliol, with Comyn. To each he would have brought his personal army, his name, his popularity, and that unique determination which led him on. If he had chosen to remain at the forefront of the struggle at this time, are we seriously to believe that he would have been rebuffed? He could not be ignored if he insisted on a leading role; he had with him veterans who were out of sympathy with the Scots lords after Falkirk and capable, unless restrained by him, of turning on those same lords. He was, in all, far from the negligible figure that is the alternative if we concede that Falkirk was as destructive of his reputation as is generally held to be the case. To the argument that neither Bruce nor Comyn would have tolerated Wallace in authority because of Falkirk one need only cite, again, the self-interest of both. Each was, and would continue to be until the murder of Comyn almost eight years later, suspicious and jealous of the other, to the extent that the adherence of Wallace must have been welcomed. An alliance with either would have offered Wallace a respectability which would have protected him if circumstances forced an accommodation with Edward. But Wallace withdrew. There is no evidence that he sought to hold on to power. He resigned and thus began that time of sacrifice which condemned him to Edward's justice.

It follows from this that Wallace had rejected the other alternative open to him, that is, of surrender to Edward. To suggest that he had ever considered the possibility is thought heresy, but no matter how unpalatable, it merits investigation. The argument that Edward would not have taken his enemy into his peace is not insuperable. At Wallace's trial in 1305 a reference to an offer of mercy by the king to Wallace was read into the indictment.[25] The approach came after Falkirk, and Edward was claiming at the trial that the prisoner had refused the offer of mercy seven years before. However hollow the proceedings were in 1305, Edward's charge may have had a foundation in fact. It is, of course, true that Edward was intent on blackening the Scot's name before judgment and on showing himself as one disposed to be reasonable to such as admitted the error of their ways and came into his peace. But in 1298 he had not yet become the violent and vicious destroyer of those who opposed him; he had not put to death Scots who defied him nor had he invoked the law of treason against them. Edward, after Falkirk, may have believed, as perhaps Bruce and Comyn did, that Wallace was a spent force; such damage as he did immediately after the battle may have been seen as a last desperate flourish. Had Edward been able to convince Wallace of the wisdom of surrender, it would have produced a greater psychological effect upon the people of Scotland than even the king himself could achieve. If mercy could be extended to Wallace, the great popular hero, and if Wallace accepted it, Edward's hold on Scotland must have been tightened. With Wallace would have come, surely, his supporters; the rift between the magnates and the lowlier members of the Scottish resistance would have widened. Wallace did not come into the English king's peace, but we do not know what form the rejection of the offer took or when he decided to continue the fight in his new role. What his frame of mind was in 1298 it is impossible to say, but he cannot entirely have escaped despair. And if he realised the futility of co-operation with the magnates, he may well have been tempted to look elsewhere in the hope of salvation for Scotland.

The theory that Wallace contemplated continuing the struggle against Edward other than militarily gains credibility when we look at the current political situation and at Wallace's own actions. He remained a convinced and committed adherent of Balliol, and in 1298 the latter's position was improving slightly. Wallace had been instrumental in securing the election of William Lamberton as bishop of St. Andrews in November 1297.[26] The bishop's devotion to the Scottish cause was not in doubt, and when he journeyed to Rome for his consecration, which took place on 1 June 1298, he would have worked hard to convince Pope Boniface VIII to seek a betterment of Balliol's situation. On his way back to Scotland, Lamberton stayed in France, where with other Scots already there he had the opportunity of gaining the ear of Philip IV. At that period, June and July 1298, when Lamberton was first in Rome then in France, both Pope and king wrote to Edward. They called on him to free Balliol and to leave Scotland in peace.[27] Although the release of Balliol was not achieved until a year later, when he passed under the protection of the papacy, Wallace would have known in 1298 of the pressure on Edward and shared in the hope of an eventual Balliol restoration. As Barrow has so clearly indicated,[28] that hope had never entirely disappeared among the Scots, and after Balliol's transfer to papal protection in 1299, it re-emerged, greatly strengthened. By his decision to go abroad in the service of Scotland, the most intriguing action of his career, Wallace was indicating a belief that the way to achieve the freedom of Scotland lay in diplomatic rather than military activity.

As with the suggestion that Wallace would ever consider surrender to Edward in 1298, the idea that he might be prepared to tolerate some kind of arrangement with him whereby Balliol would be restored as king is likely to be received with hostility. But neither the surrender nor the accommodation with Edward should be disregarded. The first would reflect Wallace's disenchantment with the magnates, the second his hope that Scotland would have its own king once more. To this end he would have gone abroad to argue for the return of Balliol. Such an event could not have been possible without the agreement of Edward; neither Wallace nor any other Scot engaged in diplomatic work could have pretended otherwise. With any such agreement would have gone conditions imposed by the English king but conditions, it might be, overseen by such independent authorities as Wallace could convince. It would not be wholly different from the situation accepted by the Scots in 1292. Why Wallace went abroad in the first place has been variously explained,[29] but all commentators are of one mind: his mission was a diplomatic one. Such a mission does not preclude the possibility that, however indirectly and however painful the thought, he and those like him were seeking just that kind of solution which would allow Balliol's restoration with Edward's agreement. Wallace was not the romantic figure he subsequently became in the popular imagination, an outlaw with the trappings so often acquired with the passage of time. He was a patriot realistic enough to understand what could be achieved and what could not. He is not diminished by the proposal that he would work for a resolution of what was otherwise an intractable problem.

If Balliol was to be restored, Edward could not be ignored. Wallace would have faced that fact with his habitual honesty. Edward was not the man to be persuaded by pope or king to give up his claim to Scotland. He saw it as both legal and valid. As Wallace knew better than most, Edward would fight for that claim. He would have been under no illusion as to the English king's determination to hold on to Scotland; nor would he have deceived himself into believing that military victory over Edward was in any way certain in the foreseeable future. But an accommodation, a restoration of Balliol under some form of English sovereignty, a buying of time – that might be another matter. Wallace was never to be deflected from his support of Balliol; he turned to diplomacy as a more subtle means of working for his restoration. It was further evidence of his honesty, of his capacity to adjust. It cannot have been easy.

There is no precise date to be given for Wallace's departure from Scotland. The incident at Peebles, touched on above, does, however, provide us with some guidance.

The events of that day in August 1299 bear relating for what they tell us of Wallace's situation and of the fragile nature of the Scottish leadership without him. A spy in the pay of Robert Hastings, Edward's constable of Roxburgh, was among the Scots present at Peebles and informed Hastings of what had happened there. Hastings in turn passed the information on to his master in a letter written on 20 August, twelve days after the developments he described: 'At the council [that is, of the Scottish leaders] Sir David Graham demanded the lands and goods of Sir William Wallace because he was leaving the kingdom without the leave or approval of the Guardians. And Sir Malcolm, Sir William's brother, answered that neither his lands nor his goods should be given away, for they were protected by the peace in which Wallace had left the kingdom, since he was leaving for the good of the kingdom. At this the two knights gave each other the lie and drew their daggers. And since Sir David Graham was of Sir John Comyn's following and Sir Malcolm Wallace of the earl of Carrick's following, it was reported to the earl of Buchan that a fight had broken out without their knowledge; and John Comyn leapt at the earl of Carrick and seized him by the throat, and the earl of Buchan turned on the bishop of St. Andrews, declaring that treason and lèsemajesté were being plotted. Eventually the Stewart and others came between them and quietened them . . . '[30]

An examination of this extract from Hastings' report is revealing. The sad fact of the recurrence of trouble between Bruce and Comyn may be passed over; little excuse was needed by either for an outbreak of violence. Although Wallace was not present at the council, we do not know why, and he had not yet gone abroad. His absence can be explained several different ways, of course. He could have been barred by those attending, although if that were the case, it would be difficult to understand Malcolm's role. He could have chosen to remain apart from his former colleagues, being disillusioned or despondent. He might have been planning his journey. He might equally by this time have fallen out of sympathy with the continuation of the war in its present form; such an attitude would be in keeping with the argument that he was now committed to a diplomatic resolution of the war. We cannot neglect the fact that, unlike Malcolm, he had played no part in the recent raid mounted by the Scots across the south of Scotland. At one time such an opportunity would have appealed to him, and one cannot but wonder that he did not participate. The raid would have been a reminder to him of those days, the year before, when, before Stirling, he had struck at Lanark, raced to Scone with Douglas to surprise Ormsby, and then hurried to assault the defences of Dundee. It may, indeed, be argued that it was precisely this sort of undertaking for which, by experience and temperament, he was most suited. Yet he did not share in it. His failure to do so unless, in contradiction of Hastings' account, he was already out of the country, is both strange and significant, indicative of his adjusting to the unfamiliar and perhaps unpalatable role he was about to play.

If, for whatever reason, Wallace was not at Peebles, his interests were well guarded. Malcolm Wallace was swift to answer on behalf of his brother and ready to protect both his name and his possessions. What Malcolm is reported to have said is not without its own interest. He asserted that his brother had left the kingdom in peace. That can only mean after Falkirk and at the time of his resignation. Malcolm's remarks may be dismissed as those to be expected of him. But that is not entirely wise. Falkirk was a defeat but it did not end the war in Edward's favour. On the contrary, even with much of the Scottish army destroyed, Edward was unable to consolidate his position, was forced to quit Scotland within two months of the battle, and would not return until July 1300. Wallace must be allowed some credit for that relatively happy state of affairs; it has not been demonstrated beyond debate that he had resigned as Guardian before Edward left Scotland in September 1298. Scotland, thus, in that sense, had been left in peace.

Lamberton, too, was at Peebles. He had returned from the Continent in time to join in the raid, and his continued devotion to Wallace is not to be questioned. According to Hastings, the earl of Buchan rounded on the bishop. Whether this implied violent intent is not clear, although it is not unlikely. Buchan saw in Lamberton a supporter of Bruce and, as Hastings makes plain, Wallace and Bruce were linked through the former's brother. Lamberton was a powerful figure in the Scottish leadership and can safely be assumed to have added his voice to that of Malcolm on behalf of Wallace on this notorious occasion. It is not easy, lacking evidence, to say the same of Bruce. He was concerned, it would appear, more with his own than with Wallace's affairs. Such words as he may have uttered in defence of Wallace would be indirect, originating in his own opposition to Comyn or to anyone who, like Graham, was associated with Comyn.

It is, of course, possible that any indifference felt by Bruce towards the absent Wallace was the result of Wallace's lack of sympathy for those now leading, since his resignation, the Scots. That lack of sympathy is borne out by Hastings. He reported to Edward that Graham had charged Wallace with leaving Scotland without permission from the Guardians. Wallace was acting as he thought fit and setting out to argue the Scottish case abroad. It makes sense therefore to believe that, once he had decided upon this journey, he was not to be deflected and did not consider the opinion of Bruce and Comyn to be of relevance or consequence. It is also reasonable to assume that he would have spoken with Lamberton before, at length, beginning his journey. If that is indeed so, he would have listened closely to what the bishop had to say on the mission, and the two would have entered into some form of agreement regarding what Wallace was to do. It is quite impossible to accept that Wallace, although enjoying an international reputation because of his achievements as Guardian, would ever go abroad without having the advantage both of Lamberton's knowledge and of written letters of introduction from him. The subordination of his natural aggression to diplomacy notwithstanding, Wallace was too strong a personality ever to be content with the humble role of messenger ascribed to him by McNair Scott, but he would not have neglected to insist on the blessing and the fullest support of the Church, through his constant friend and ally Lamberton, and no doubt also through Wishart. That enigmatic figure, whatever the vagaries of his relationship with Wallace, cannot have done other than wish for the success of the forthcoming mission.

At some unrecorded date, either about the time of or soon after the meeting at Peebles, Wallace left Scotland for the Continent. Again, interestingly, we find ourselves deprived of precise details of his movements and his activities. If he does not entirely disappear, he fades, not from the popular memory, but from the accounts of the chroniclers. Such slight information as we have suggests that he may have visited Norway, France, and Rome, probably in that order, and if we despair of learning the truth we can, as always, turn to Blind Harry to elaborate on Wallace's adventures – for such they must have been – with his customary invention. Thus, if Harry is to be believed, Wallace fought with the French pirate, Thomas Longueville the Red Rover, who, recognising superior virtue as much as strength, became his companion, and with the Englishman, Thomas Lyn, not to mention his epic defeat of an enraged lion. Major[31] is not alone in questioning Harry's fabrications, but in the course of his extended wanderings Wallace would most certainly have had the opportunity of proving his courage in the simple interest of staying alive. Why, therefore, should not Philip IV have sought to enlist Wallace in his service, as the tradition would have us believe? Philip was nothing if not intelligent; an ally of the experience and stature of Wallace was not to be overlooked. That same tradition has the Scot decline the honour, and the rewards of serving the king of France for that love of country which was, finally, to destroy him, but we cannot confidently state that Wallace was not approached by Philip or his agents.

The evidence for a visit by Wallace to Norway lies in a safe-conduct issued to him in the name of Haakon V. This document, together with others of perhaps greater significance, was found on Wallace's person at the time of his arrest by Menteith[32] but, like them, has disappeared. Whether Wallace met Haakon we do not know, and what such a meeting, if ever it took place, was intended to achieve is equally unclear. Certainly, any kind of military alliance between Scotland and Norway was unlikely if not impossible. Norway would remain for some considerable time, as it had always been, an important if unreliable factor in Scottish politics. Had not Eric II, father of the Maid, been among the original competitors for the throne of Scotland, no matter how insubstantial his claim? The battle of Largs and the treaty of Perth both lay well within living memory. Not until 1468 would Shetland and Orkney become part of the Scottish kingdom. The Scots, however desperate they thought their situation at the time of Wallace's departure, would not have sought to bring to their shores a Norwegian force whose friendship could never be taken for granted, even if Haakon had been willing to supply it. It may be that, as Barrow suggests,[33] Wallace went no further into the possessions of the king of Norway than the Orkneys; such a journey would still have entailed a safe-conduct. Wallace would in any case be more drawn to Germany than to Norway, to those towns such as Hamburg and Lübeck with which he had been anxious to establish contact in the course of his association with Murray. There is no reference to his going to Germany, but such a visit makes at least as much sense as one to Norway. If indeed he went to Germany, he would first have gone north in order to lessen the possibility of interception and capture by the English whose ships would have rendered hazardous a crossing of the North Sea by the direct route. Wallace would have been anxious to convince any German towns which he did in fact visit of the continued wisdom of trade with a Scotland still independent of England. [34]

We can speak with more authority when we turn to the question of Wallace and France. That he came to the attention of Philip IV is indisputable, although the exact circumstances seem to puzzle the chroniclers who tell us of the vicissitudes suffered by Wallace at this time. One account has him seized with his companions on the orders of the French king who was ready to turn him over to Edward. [35] Wallace may here have been the victim of a temporary cessation of the feud between the two kings from which the Scots had for so long sought to benefit. In June of 1299 at Montreuil-sur-Mer a treaty was agreed for the marriage of Edward with Philip's sister, Margaret, which took place on 4 September. Edward, in thanking Philip, merely asked him to retain Wallace in France, a peculiar circumstance to which it will be necessary to return. [36] Whether or not Wallace subsequently impressed Philip by deeds such as those Blind Harry describes, the French king proved to be not unsympathetic to the Scot. Devious as he was, Philip was not the man to allow the marriage of his sister to interfere for long with his quarrel with Edward, and almost four years were to pass before Philip made with Edward that treaty which helped to break the Scottish resistance to Edward. In the meantime, Philip had Wallace in France, a possible source of embarrassment to Edward. It is not beyond the bounds of possibility that he was as impressed by Wallace as Blind Harry would have it, but Wallace was not to be seduced from his mission. On his behalf Philip wrote to Rome to instruct the French representatives at the court of Boniface to aid Wallace, whom he chooses to describe as 'our beloved William le Walois of Scotland knight', in the work he was about to undertake there. [37] Philip's letter is dated 7 November 1300 and therefore heralds Wallace's departure for Rome. What he hoped to achieve there it is difficult to say, for he was about to become involved in a debate of a kind for which he was eminently unsuited, in what was in essence a trial of the question of Scotland before the papal court. [38] At the time at which Philip's letter was written, Wallace had been away from Scotland for more than a year. It cannot have been an easy year for him but, as was his way, he sacrificed himself to the cause of Scotland wherever that cause took him. In his absence, Bruce had resigned the Guardianship, Edward had invaded Scotland in a campaign from which neither he nor the Scots could claim great satisfaction, and a truce of seven months had been agreed. To these and other events in Scotland we must now turn.

NOTES

1. Cf. Kightly: *Folk Heroes of Britain*, 181; R. McNair Scott: *Robert the Bruce King of Scots*, 53; Barrow: *Robert Bruce*, 146; Barron: *Scottish War of Independence*, 84.

2. Fordun, 102.

3. See chap. 6 above. The role of Bruce at Falkirk has never been satisfactorily explained. It is perhaps significant that both Barrow, and Bruce's most recent biographer, McNair Scott, seek to avoid the question.

4. Wright: *Political Songs*, 176.

5. Barbour: *Bruce*, 234; *Scalacronicon*, 142-3.

6. Major, Book IV, chap. XIV.

7. Major, Book VIII, chap. XXVIII.

8. Cf. Barrow, 146-7; Kightly, 181.

9. Rishanger, 387; Pluscarden, Book VIII, chap. XXVIII.

10. Fordun, 101.

11. Pluscarden, Book VIII, chap. XXVIII.

12. Book IV, chap. XIV.

13. Rishanger, 187.

14. Rishanger, 188.

15. Major, Book IV, chap. XIV.

16. Rishanger, 188.

17. Rishanger, 387.

18. Kightly, 181.

19. Barrow: *Robert Bruce*, 146.

20. See chap. 4 above.

21. The small force of cavalry had fled; the Comyn faction, according to Fordun, had deserted; what Bruce did is unclear; Wallace himself left the field.

22. On the development of the Guardianship, see N. Reid: 'The Kingless Kingdom: the Scottish Guardianships of 1286-1306', *S.H.R.* LXI, 2, no. 172, 1982.

23. McNair Scott, 53.

24. Barrow: *Robert Bruce*, 147.

25. See chap. 10 below.

26. See chap. 5 above.

27. Rishanger, 185.

28. *Robert Bruce*, chap. 6.

29. Kightly (182) sees his mission as of his own making; McNair Scott (53) makes him Lamberton's messenger to France; Barrow, *Robert Bruce*, 165, recognises that his work abroad was more important.

30. *Cal. Doc. Scot.*, ii, 1978, in Public Record Office, London.

31. Major, Book IV, chap. XIV.

32. See Barrow: *Robert Bruce*, 164 n. 4.

33. Barrow, 164.

34. Barrow, 14-15, traces briefly the German interest in trade with Scotland.

35. Rishanger, 387.

36. See chap. 10.

37. Stevenson: *Documents Illustrative of Sir William Wallace, his Life and Times*, 163.

38. On the proceedings in Rome, see Barrow: *Bruce*, 166-9; Barrow: *Kingdom*, 244-5; McNair Scott, 59 and 241-2.

CHAPTER 8

The Time of Doubt, 1303-1304

The date of Wallace's return to Scotland from the work he had undertaken on the Continent is not known. We have to wait for the campaign of 1303 to 1304 for convincing proof that he was back in his own country and engaged against the English.[1] If it is difficult to see him, a patriot of patriots, remaining abroad for longer than absolutely necessary to carry out the task of helping in the presentation of the Scottish case, the argument of a recent writer[2] that he participated with Robert Bruce in a force dispatched by bishop Wishart, his former colleague, to fight against the English in the south-west in the late summer and autumn of 1301 is open to question. Wallace was still in Scotland, according to the letter from Robert Hastings to Edward to which reference has already been made, as late as August 1299.[3] From another source we learn that he had been responsible for cutting off supplies to the English garrison of Stirling Castle on the twenty-fourth of that same month.[4] His travels on the Continent, even if we limit them to France and Rome and thus ignore the possibility that he reached the Baltic and Norway, were nevertheless extensive. His embassy to the Papal Court could not be hurried. There is no cause to add the adventures which Blind Harry finds for him while he was in France[5] to appreciate that Wallace's stay on the Continent is likely to have been as little as two years. We can only assert with any hope of accuracy that he would not hesitate to make his way back to Scotland to renew his and his country's struggle against Edward I at the earliest possible moment.

When he did return, it was to a subordinate position in a Scotland different from the one he had left. The balance of power had shifted and the ordering of affairs was in other and, in terms of the Guardianship, new hands. If Wallace was unique in his achievements, he was not, of course, unique in his devotion to the independence of Scotland. The armies which he led at Stirling and more particularly at Falkirk were filled with men of like persuasion. Unnamed and in any other context viewed as unimportant, they were ready to lay down their lives at his command. They stood to the end of Falkirk, helpless against the missiles and the cavalry attack. Alongside them, if not always in battle at least possessing a special kind of expertise in government, must be placed those without whom independence was impossible to accomplish. It was with them that authority had resided since Wallace's decision to resign from the Guardianship. Superior to him in origins and social class and often lacking his resolution, they followed their own path, parallel to his but sometimes crossing it. They it was who carried out the complicated diplomatic manoeuvres and maintained the government of Scotland as the response to Edward's repeated assaults upon Scotland.

By the beginning of 1301 necessity had forced the Scots to accept that a return to the concept of a single Guardian was unavoidable. The combination of Bruce and Comyn, already noted,[6] could not survive the clash of personalities and ambitions and did not. The addition of bishop Lamberton, Wallace's choice for the see of St. Andrews in 1297, to the combination of Bruce and Comyn could only delay the inevitable. Comyn held on to office while Bruce chose resignation. Whether Bruce, in resigning, was planning that defection to the English which ultimately took place in January or February of 1302 is unclear. As long as Balliol retained that place, however unjustified by his person or by events, which made his restoration the continued obsession behind Scottish diplomacy, the defection of Bruce was a matter of time. Ingram de Umfraville replaced Bruce as Guardian on 10 May 1300 at the parliament of Rutherglen, but the triumvirate which he formed with Comyn and Lamberton did not last a year.

If the Scots then concluded that they must select a sole Guardian because dissension prevented an alternative, there was no outstanding candidate. Comyn's apparent failure to work with others was open to criticism, while his conduct at Falkirk must still have rankled. Bruce was not free of the suspicion of inconstancy and personal ambition. He would in any case be opposed by Comyn, as he himself would have opposed the other man. Umfraville had a long and distinguished career in the war but, in the context of the Guardianship, did not match the standing of Bruce and Comyn. Lamberton, as a bishop, was unlikely to be considered. Wallace, the first sole Guardian and despite Falkirk neither forgotten nor disregarded by the people, had disqualified himself and was absent on the Continent. It would be idle to suppose that, had he been in Scotland, he would have been considered by those whose voices carried most weight; he had been relegated, as far as they were concerned, to the lower ranks.

We are ignorant of the process of selection and of the means by which the choice of John de Soules was arrived at. If he emerged as Guardian as a compromise, he should not be undervalued. Soules was a moderate in the sense that he was not bound to the Bruce or the Comyn faction. If his name appeared as one of the auditors acting for Robert Bruce the Competitor in

the protracted search for a king after the death of Margaret of Norway, he
was to maintain a certain distance from the family's later activities. It is
true that he did not escape future censure,[7] but the source of that censure,
the chronicler Fordun, was not impartial. Soules' relationship, through the
marriage of his nephew into the Comyn family, with John Comyn, Bruce's
opponent, surely counted more with Fordun than it did with those who
sought a Guardian for Scotland in early 1301. It has been written of this
neglected, virtually unknown man[8] that his 'record of constancy in the
patriot cause can stand beside that of Wallace'. Given Wallace's unshake-
able hold on the public imagination and Soules' relative anonymity, that
statement, however reasoned, is not well supported. Unquestionably, he
made no impact comparable to that of Wallace. But of the period 1296 to
1305, it might be said that no one did. Soules made no end as a martyr on an
English scaffold as did his more celebrated contemporary. But if Soules
died quietly, it was as an exile in France, a determined fighter for Scotland.
How he was seen by the English can be deduced from their treatment of
him when, with Wallace and Simon Fraser, he refused to submit to
Edward in 1304. If Soules, unlike Wallace, was not pursued to the death by
Edward, Edward nevertheless appears to have looked on him as one of the
more dangerous of his Scottish opponents. At this time, Edward, although
generally in a conciliatory mood, decreed that 'The Stewart, Sir John de
Soules and Sir Ingram de Umfraville are not to have safe conducts nor
come within the king's power until Sir William Wallace is given up'.[9]
Unlike the Stewart and Umfraville, Soules stubbornly refused to come
into Edward's peace, a stance of which Wallace, with whom his connection
is evident from Edward's decree, would have approved.

Wallace and Soules, then, were both the victims of the relentless, almost
pathological, hostility of Edward I. It is an intriguing thought that that
monarch, to whom the motto *Pactum serva* or 'keep faith' has been
ascribed, failed so signally to see its virtue in others. For him the character
of Robert Bruce, that most inconstant of men, was more appealing. In him
perhaps he recognised himself. He forgave Bruce where he could not bring
himself to let Wallace live or grant Soules his peace other than on
conditions which he must have known Soules would reject. As they shared
the enmity of the English kind, so did Wallace and Soules share the belief
that the independence of Scotland was linked inexorably with the restoration of Balliol. They maintained to the end that it was for the Scots
themselves to choose to keep or replace that pathetic man. Although Soules
from his exile in France would later support Bruce when the latter had
murdered Comyn and made himself king, he was Balliol's man while
Balliol lived. In this his constancy was the equal of Wallace's own. We may

doubt the wisdom of their continued allegiance to Balliol. He was not a man to inspire devotion. He had lost his throne in the most ignominious of ways and, once removed from Scotland, was content to allow others to risk their lives and lands on his behalf. But Wallace and Soules were not romantics. They were under no illusions as to the Balliol's quality. Hardheaded and practical, they saw in Balliol a symbol of choice and therefore of freedom.

Under the Guardianship of Soules the Scottish efforts to secure the restoration of Balliol were intensified. At Rome, to which Wallace had made his way, the papacy had continued in the person of Boniface VIII that policy of sympathetic understanding of the Scottish cause which dated at least as far back as the year 1294. This was in large part due to the debating skill of the Scottish delegation which, with one Master Baldred Bissett an exceptional advocate, made such an impression at the papal court. It was from Soules that this delegation, of which it is possible Wallace was a member, derived its authority.[10] The Scots, confident that their success over Edward's representatives at Rome was an important step towards the return to Scotland of Balliol, appeared to have deceived themselves into thinking that Edward would concede it. He had, of course, no such intention. Certainly, he would never allow Balliol or any other king of Scotland to rule without imposing his own conditions. But there is no evidence that he had any concession in mind. Soules and the Scots could argue as they would, Edward would be bound by no will other than his own.

The Scots under Soules were faced by the unpleasant fact that only the death of Edward was likely to end the war. There was no sign of that in 1301. In the summer he campaigned in Scotland with his usual vigour but with as little success as in the previous year. He brought with him his son, Prince Edward, to whom he entrusted the submission of the south-west. It was the king's wish, it is said,[11] that the prince should have 'the chief honour of taming the pride of the Scots'. The prince was as unsuccessful as his father but learned something of his intransigence. Edward spent the winter of 1301 to 1302 at Linlithgow, but if it was his capital, he was in no sense the master of Scotland. Soules knew better than to offer Edward the opportunity of a decisive battle, but his tactics of harassment wore the English down and Edward was forced to agree to a truce of nine months on 26 January 1302.

The truce had not rid Scotland of the English presence. Nor could it have any effect on two significant events of 1302. Bruce defected to the English, the possibility of the restoration of Balliol no doubt a strong factor in his calculations.[12] If that is so, it says much for the power of Scottish propaganda both in Rome and at the court of Philip of France, into whose custody Balliol had been released in the summer of the previous year. Bruce, a realistic man when compared to such as Wallace, must have been affected by the general Scottish mood. What damage his defection did to the Scottish cause it is impossible precisely to say. It must, certainly, have been a counter to the Scottish propaganda and it made Edward's position in the south-west easier.

More serious for Scotland was the change in the fortunes of Philip of France which occurred after his defeat at Courtrai in July. The arrogance of the French nobility was as great as that of the Scots and, as at Dunbar, produced the same outcome if with greater slaughter. Thereafter Philip was less able to support the Scots, even if he had wished to. Unsentimental as he was, the French king, also distracted by his notorious embroilment with the papacy, was looking with a less sympathetic eye than before. He had to assess what the Scots could offer; it is not surprising that he saw no profit in the alliance with them. Soules did not fail to recognise the danger and himself went to France in the autumn. With Lamberton, James the Stewart and Umfraville, among others, he argued in vain. If Rome in 1301 was a happy arena for the Scots, Paris in 1302 was not. The interests of France alone dictated Philip's answer.

On 20 May 1303, a treaty of peace was signed between France and England at Paris and ratified on 10 July by Edward, who was then at Perth. Scotland, excluded from the treaty, was open to him. Hostilities had resumed with the end of the nine-month truce and Edward had wasted no time in ordering his lieutenant in Scotland, Sir John Segrave (later to bring the captured and doomed Wallace to London), into action. It is with these events that Wallace once more enters the picture. What he had been doing since his work on the Continent we do not know and it is, simply, idle to speculate. For one English chronicler of the period, however,[13] there is no doubt as to his role. Wallace, 'their commander and captain', was at the head of the Scots. This is plainly incorrect. He could not re-emerge in authority. With Soules in France, affairs in Scotland had passed into the hands of John Comyn,[14] the former Guardian who assumed the position for a second time. It is not credible that Comyn should have allowed Wallace the position with which Rishanger credits him. Enemies they may not have been, but Comyn, as at Falkirk, was no admirer of Wallace. That apart, as well as Wallace's suspicion of Comyn, again the legacy of Falkirk, there is no record of any achievement by Wallace since his resignation of the Guardianship which could, in military terms, have entitled him to command. He had passed from the forefront if not from the minds of the people.

This is not to say that he did not throw himself into the struggle and that he did not, by example, animate the Scottish resistance. He would always do that. But, again, it is difficult to allot him a precise place in what was happening. It is impossible to state categorically that he was present at the success the Scots achieved at Roslin on February 24 1303.[15] Sir John Segrave, on the instructions of his king who was still not ready to assume command in person in Scotland, was leading a large force of cavalry on a reconnaissance to test the Scottish strength west of Edinburgh when he was set upon by Scottish troops. These, mounted, had come from Biggar in an action which bore the hallmark of Wallace. Learning of the English advance, they had scorned the darkness and surprised Segrave, whose force suffered badly in the attack.[16] A number of English knights were killed, more were captured, and Segrave himself, at the head of the first brigade of horse, was badly wounded. If he was rescued soon enough, he had almost met with disgrace. But Wallace was not the leader of this Scottish attack. If he took part, it was under the command of the Guardian, John Comyn, and Simon Fraser. Roslin was not a victory, it made no great difference to the course of events, but it proved that in the tactics of which Wallace was such a master lay the best chance of success for the Scots.

The arrival of Edward himself in Scotland, as so often, swung control of the war away from the Scots. He had summoned his host for May and by the middle of that month had crossed the Border. He was at Roxburgh on 16 May, Ascension Day. He again gave his son a command in the south-west. With the prince went Richard de Burgh, earl of Ulster, Robert Bruce's father-in-law. Edward moved through the east of Scotland in what was a copy of his progress of 1296. Although it was less of a formality than on the previous occasion, he met little resistance. He had chosen to avoid Stirling with its castle, held by Sir William Oliphant, another of those lesser but still worthy Scots who defied Edward almost to the death. Edward was a master of detail, prepared to employ whatever methods were best suited to his purpose. His army was able to cross the Firth of Forth and thus bypass Stirling on three prefabricated bridges which he had ferried up the east coast from King's Lynn. In the following year he would take Stirling with the help of siege engines which the Scots were never able to match. Of course Edward had to find the money for these and the other massive expenses which this and similar campaigns entailed. Edward could never forget this, nor was he allowed to by the magnates and the clergy upon whom he had continued to make the kind of demands which had brought civil war close in the period before Falkirk. Edward could never entirely reconcile himself to the fact that the Scots were as determined as he, and he therefore found an excuse for his failures in Scotland in the shortage of ready money. He had made plain when he wrote in 1301 to the exchequer: 'And you can be certain that if it had not been for a lack of money we would have finished the bridge which was started to cross the Scottish Sea and you must understand for sure that if we had been able to cross this season, we would have achieved such an exploit against our enemies that our business in these parts would have been brought to a good and honourable conclusion in a short time'.[17]

The conquest of Scotland would have offered Edward a partial solution to his financial problems. His failure to achieve that conquest may in part explain his growing impatience and, ultimately, violence. But in 1303, if he could not forget the need for money, he was able to enjoy his progress through Scotland. Only at Brechin, where he arrived at the end of July, did he face serious opposition.[18] Barron tells us that he found the castles of Urquhart and Cromarty defiant and their capture involved heavy fighting.[19] Edward was at Kinloss in September and then returned to Dumfermline, intending to winter there.

It is impossible to say if Wallace was able to make any attempt to interfere with Edward's progress through the eastern half of Scotland. There is little likelihood that he did, for he had retired into the Forest of Selkirk, so often his lair in the past. The dangers involved in an assault on the powerful and confident army which Edward commanded were too great. The territory over which Wallace would have had to travel to carry out an attack was held by the English. The shelter of the forest, with the opportunity it offered for regrouping and planning away from the threat of harassment by the enemy could not be ignored. Wallace, therefore, now returned to that form of warfare by which he had first made his name, the raid.

The long-established belief, to which Trevelyan, among others, gave expression, that 'Wallace was a guerrilla leader of genius',[20] has been challenged with great authority by Barrow.[21] Wallace's use of large armies, at Stirling and Falkirk, appears to support Barrow's argument. The skill with which he trained and then handled these armies in battle shows that he was confident in the set-piece. But he was adept in the command of the smaller as well as of the larger unit. Stirling and Falkirk are evidence of his talent for improvisation rather than of that conservatism of which Barrow writes. It was a talent which he shared with his enemy, Edward I. However meticulous his preparations, Edward excelled in the change of direction, the shift of emphasis, the taking advantage of an opening. He did not defeat the Scots at Falkirk because of his attention to detail. He could not even dictate the course of the battle; his subordinates disregarded him, if they did not disobey him. He did, however, see the weakness of the Scots once the cavalry had fled, and he did not hesitate to bring into action the one branch of his army to which the Scots now had no answer. It may be that genius in war lies in that one quality which Wallace and Edward had in common. In 1303 Wallace was denied an army. He therefore did not neglect the tactics of the guerrilla any more than he had in an earlier stage of the war. Since Falkirk the Scots, wisely, had not used the call to arms which produced a large and, if badly handled, an unwieldy force. For Wallace there was no alternative to the raid.

We thus find him issuing from the forest to strike into Annandale and Liddesdale and as far south as Cumberland. He was not, however, in sole control of the considerable force of infantry and horse which was employed on this occasion.[22] The raid of June 1303 is of interest for two particular reasons: the leadership and the intention behind the sortie. With Wallace were associated Comyn and Fraser. In them Wallace was working with two men as unshaken as he in their devotion to the cause of Balliol. It is important to emphasise that their devotion was to that cause, for by this time they did not share Wallace's own attitude to the continuation of the war as such. Balliol, especially after the Anglo-Franch treaty of 20 May, no longer had any realistic hope of restoration. He himself had settled for a life of retreat, far from the scene of action, and might not have welcomed a return to Scotland. Comyn and Fraser knew this; their submission to Edward was a matter of time. Comyn was still in arms in the autumn, a threat to the English but a reduced one. Like Bruce, he was not a simple man but as inclined as his opponent to consider his own future. Whether he, again like Bruce, had ambitions to replace Balliol as king, albeit under Edward's tutelage, is a mystery, but he saw himself as second to none in the Scottish hierarchy. Fraser died in 1306 and, if he is remembered at all, it is as a Scottish martyr. But he could never match Wallace's resolution. As recently as 1300 he had fought on the English side at the siege and capture of Caerlaverock. His subsequent move into the Scottish camp was never forgotten or forgiven by Edward, whose terms to Fraser were severe. Were Comyn and Fraser at the time of the raid already considering submission? There is no means of answering that question. But the raid was the final throw of the Balliol party, so strongly represented by Wallace, Comyn and Fraser.

If Wallace and his colleagues hoped by their raid into Cumberland to force Edward to turn to its defence and thus relieve the pressure on Scotland, their secondary task must have been to punish Bruce for his defection by striking at his home territory of Annandale. Bruce's value to the English cause in 1303 and 1304 was not merely one of propaganda. Even those who argue for him must concede that he was active in Edward's service.[23] Comyn therefore, for his part, did not need the excuse of a family feud to attack Annandale. As for Wallace, we can assume that he saw in the raid a legitimate method of exacting revenge upon one whom he would consider a traitor. It was not in his nature to equivocate when the question was one of loyalty to Scotland. He applied throughout his career one elementary test, and that Bruce had failed.

The raid, of course, did not succeed in its primary aim. In that respect, if not desperate, it was from the beginning hopeless. Edward was not to be diverted; in his present campaign lay the best chance of the final subjugation since 1296. In May, despite the blow of the Anglo-French treaty, the Scots, at least those in Paris, were optimistic enough to believe that Edward might again concede a truce.[24] Such an attitude was ill-conceived and ill-founded. The facts argued against it. Edward swept through the east, Bruce was his man, Comyn was beginning to weaken. However volatile he might be, Edward was always capable of patience when, as in late 1303, he could see an end in sight. He waited, secure in the knowledge that those who had defied him would, at length, come to him. He was not a cynical man, rather an experienced one. He could categorise the Scots with a fair degree of accuracy and had done so from the start of the proceedings to find a king of Scotland. Wallace, unlike the others, defied Edward's calculations.

He would have no part in the negotiations which led to the general Scottish submission in February 1304. He may have been strengthened in his resolve by outside influences. At various stages throughout the long war the Scots showed themselves capable of the most sublime sentiments, expressed in letters and documents. If the most celebrated example is to be found in the Declaration of Arbroath, there were others too often overlooked. One such was a letter written on 25 May 1303 on behalf of the Scottish delegation then in Paris with the thankless and fruitless task of dissuading Philip IV from an alliance with England.[25] We do not know who was responsible for the drafting of the letter, whether it was Soules or Lamberton, or, no less likely in the circumstances, a clerk imbued with their spirit but better able to put their thoughts into words. The letter urges constancy and offers hope. To those for whom it was destined it said: 'For God's sake do not despair. If you have ever done brave deeds, do braver ones now. The swiftest runner who fails before the winning-post has run in vain'. These words might have been written *of* Wallace rather than *for* him and those who persevered with him. The letter may never have come to his notice, but how appropriate it was. Tragically, he would fail well before the winning-post, but by that failure he did prove the letter wrong. In late 1303 and early 1304, as Comyn and the other leaders of

Scottish resistance were seeking first a respite and then to come into Edward's peace, he did not swerve from his duty and the task he had set himself. The claim by one English chronicler that Wallace sought terms at the beginning of 1304 does not ring true. The reason is not one based on emotion but on one element of the supposed approach to Edward. Wallace, we are to believe, requested of Edward, through intermediaries, that he be allowed to 'submit to his honest peace without surrendering into his hands body or head'. This is a standard formula. It is when we consider the words which the chronicler puts into Wallace's mouth that we are forced to dismiss the possibility that Wallace really meant to submit. Wallace, in this account, was either so naive or so arrogant that he proposed that 'the king grant him of his gift, not as a loan, an honourable allowance of woods and cattle and by his writing the seizure and investment for him and his heirs in purchased land'. Not surprisingly, Edward is reported to have been affronted and offered a reward for the death of Wallace. The Wallace we read of here, the Wallace who is also supposed to have made a similar plea to come into Edward's peace the previous year,[26] is neither the Wallace of history nor of tradition.

He was now increasingly alone and isolated. Edward had not wavered in his determination to take him. We cannot put a date to Edward's decision that Wallace should not be pardoned. It may have been as early as Lanark. Stirling and the destructive raid into the north of England which followed the battle would add to the enormity of Wallace's crimes. Yet it is possible, as the indictment of 1305 relates,[27] that after Falkirk Edward was willing to accept Wallace into his peace. Furthermore, the English king, as has been seen,[28] turned down Philip IV's offer to surrender Wallace to him. Wallace's reappearance on the Scottish side in 1303 after his embassy on the Continent, and in despite of what Edward took to be his generosity, may have shaped the king's future attitude.

Edward used whatever means came to hand in his pursuit of Wallace. Those who hunted down the Scots were guaranteed reward; Edward did not expect his helpers to have high motives. Something of this emerges from an undated document from the period of 1297 to 1303. The document, as becomes clear, carries a sting in the tail: 'The king by his letters patent grants to his chier vadlet Edward de Keith, all goods and chattels of whatever kind he may gain from Monsire Guilliam le Galeys [Wallace] the King's enemy, to his own profit and pleasure. Provided, however, that if the said Edward by chance under colour of this gift takes anything from other people at the King's peace, he shall duly answer to those from whom such are taken'.[29] The king did not deceive himself, then, as to the quality of those he employed, but he himself was not swayed by niceties. To capture Wallace he would scorn no opportunity, send away no man who offered his services. The number of these increased with the submission of 1304.

Edward spent the months of November 1303 to February 1304 at Dunfermline with his second wife, the Frenchwoman Margaret. There he was accessible to the many Scots who now sought to make their peace with him. He was more gracious, in this hour of triumph, than he had been in another, in 1296. His son, less than successful in the south-west in the summer and autumn, had established himself at Perth by Christmas, and it was to him that Edward entrusted the negotiations for the Scottish surrender, for such it was. Comyn, still technically Guardian and in the absence of Soules the obvious choice for the distasteful task, acted for the Scots. Edward was disposed to be generous, even tolerant; the statesman-like qualities so much admired in the past had not entirely deserted him. He could afford to indulge the Scots; he was their master and they knew it. But, nevertheless, Comyn conducted himself with an authority and a confidence surprising to us, given the circumstances. He was not Balliol, nor was he required to be. Neither he nor those he represented would be stripped of honour and dignity. Edward understood and accepted that there was no question of unconditional surrender. He knew the importance of this concession if he was to gain and keep the support of the Scots for his plan for their country.

On 9 February Comyn, with eleven associates, surrendered at Strathord near Perth. The terms which he had been able to obtain from Edward need not concern us here.[30] Wallace was not among those who submitted to Edward. He had excluded himself from the negotiations and was, in turn, with Soules and Fraser, excluded from the terms accepted by Comyn. There is no indication in any source that Comyn or Bruce or any of the Scottish leaders now in Edward's peace interceded for his life. Even Robert Wishart, the bishop of Glasgow, said by the English to have been the instigator of Wallace's first actions, did not speak up for him at this moment of reconciliation with the English king. Wishart was not a young man, his courage did not always stand the test, and he was still viewed with suspicion by Edward, who insisted on his brief exile. Lamberton and James the Stewart, the one Wallace's appointee, the other his feudal superior, returned from France to make their peace. No doubt they were, like others, glad to have it. No doubt they could claim that no one was capable of influencing Edward's attitude towards Wallace. The sad fact remains that the Scottish leaders now in Scotland cannot be exonerated of the charge of, at best, indifference to Wallace, with whom they had served and with whose sentiments they had claimed to sympathise. In the eighteen months left to Wallace after the surrender at Starthord, we can find no evidence that his former colleagues, some of them friends, made one positive move to save him from the fate which became increasingly inevitable once Edward was free to concentrate on him. They made no intervention at Edward's court, they entered no plea, they offered no bargain, and at the end they cannot satisfactorily be cleared of possible complicity, through their neglect if for no other reason, in his death. They left him to Edward. A foretaste of what that could mean came with the fall to the English of Stirling Castle.

NOTES

1. *D.N.B.* 568-9 deals, briefly, with his possible movements.
2. Kightly, 183.
3. Chap. 7 above.
4. *Cal. Docs. Scot.*, ii, 1949.
5. Ninth book.
6. Chap. 7 above.
7. Fordun, i. 331.
8. Barrow: *Robert Bruce*, 162.
9. *Docs. Illus. Hist. Scot.* 276.
10. On the delegation see Barrow: *Robert Bruce*, 166ff.
11. *Cal. Docs. Scot.*, ii, 1191.
12. He had, of course, never accepted Balliol as king. On his motives see Barrow: *Robert Bruce*, 172-5, and McNair Scott, 60-61.
13. Rishanger.
14. Wallace's relationship with Comyn is as difficult to judge as that with Bruce. Comyn, of course, suffered, as Bruce did not, from Scottish chroniclers, but in his apparent dislike of Wallace he cannot have been unique, any more than in his wish to see him toppled.
15. He would undoubtedly have been mentioned had he been present, especially in the light of Rishanger's comment.
16. Fordun, i. 333-5.
17. q. Prestwich, 50.
18. *Cal. Docs. Scot.*, ii, 1687, 1386.
19. Barron, 193.
20. *History of England*, 1945, 218.
21. *Robert Bruce*, 130.
22. *Cal. Docs. Scot.*, ii, 1374.
23. He was in charge of the garrison of Ayr and took part in the attack on the Scots at Peebles.
24. Lamberton, for example, wrote to Wallace to encourage him. *Docs. Illus. Hist. Scot.*, 333.

25. q. Barrow: *Robert Bruce*, 180.

26. Bellamy: *The Law of Treason in England in the Later Middle Ages*, 1970, 33, deals with the question of Wallace's approaches to Edward.

27. See chap. 10 below.

28. See above, p. 98.

29. *Cal. Docs. Scot.*, ii, 1424.

30. *Foedera*, i. 974-5.

CHAPTER 9

The Time of Betrayal, 1305

Stirling Castle was held for the Scots by a young, and as Edward was to learn in the summer of 1304, a courageous man.' Sir William Oliphant, however, appears to have been guided by a different, more esoteric code than that to which Wallace subscribed. That is not in any way to decry his contribution to the cause of independence through his defiance of Edward. That cause, like any other, needed heroes, even martyrs; Oliphant was the former and came near to being the latter. Two incidents, however, illustrate that not all Scots were motivated in the same way as Wallace, yet their role cannot be disregarded. The submission of February freed Edward to carry out what might nowadays be called mopping-up operations. One such, albeit a great undertaking, was the siege of Stirling.

The castle had been left alone by Edward in the campaign of 1303. It stood as a stronghold but, perhaps of more moment to Edward, it represented through Oliphant's stubborn refusal to surrender the kind of obstacle to Edward's total subjection of Scotland which Wallace personified. When he began the siege of Stirling in May 1304, therefore, Edward was not in a mood to be tolerant of any opposition. In a move which strikes us today as strange, Oliphant asked for permission to seek the advice of Sir John Soules who, as Guardian, had put the care of the castle into his hands.[1] Oliphant required to know of Soules whether he was to fight or surrender. It is Edward's refusal which has attracted comment.[2] Yet, it is impossible to see Wallace, in like circumstances, communicating with Edward, let alone contemplating an alternative to defiance. One has only to think of his words to English emissaries before Stirling to see the point proved.[3] But Oliphant was a man of great heart; he subscribed to a set of values which had no place in the reasoning of Wallace.

Oliphant's later career offers a further example of this. After the fall of Stirling he was a prisoner of the English until 1308. He obtained his freedom by agreeing to fight for Edward II against Robert I.[4] In October 1311 he was in command of the English garrison of Perth. It was at Perth that one part of the dismembered body of Wallace was displayed. Thus two Scots – Oliphant was a Perthshire man – had, with others, defied Edward. Now one fought on the English side, and was in no way condemned by

113

contemporary chroniclers for doing so. The other died for the same cause
that the first had embraced and, then, to save his life, deserted. Oliphant
had been a Balliol man but that did not deter him when once again he
changed sides to become a supporter of Bruce. Wallace was incapable of
such thinking; it is likely he despised it. But in the summer of 1304 he and
Oliphant were comrades.

It took Edward three months to capture Stirling. He used the siege to
experiment with the most advanced technology of the age. His favourite
weapon against the castle and its garrison was the machine known as
'Warwolf', against which the Scots had no defence. On July 20 the garrison
was allowed to surrender after Edward had used the castle with them inside
for a day's target practice for 'Warwolf'. Edward was only dissuaded from
hanging and disembowelling them by the intervention of those about him,
notably his wife.[5] Oliphant and the survivors of the siege were sent to
England, to various prisons. Not even the English themselves could
forgive Edward for his intentions.

Edward's treatment of Oliphant and the Stirling garrison could leave no
further doubt of the reception which awaited Wallace upon capture.
Edward had been guilty at Stirling of a breach of that code of chivalry
which, like Oliphant, he claimed to hold dear. To act so, Edward must have
been dominated by an extreme passion. It came, perhaps, from frustration,
from that rage which he had inherited from his Plantagenet forebears, from
inherent defects at which we can only guess from these and other sources.
While it would be foolish indeed to eliminate these from the attempt to
explain his behaviour towards Wallace, it may well be that Edward was
colder, more controlled in his pursuit and execution of Wallace than is
generally believed. Certainly, as will be argued,[6] the trial of Wallace was
not merely contrived but directed by a man not swayed by emotion alone.

It would be easy, that is, to see in Edward no more than the anointed
guardian of that hatred of Wallace which is found in popular form in, for
example, Lanercost:

> The vilest doom is fittest for thys crimes,
> Justice demands that thou shouldst die three times.
> Thou pillager of many a sacred shrine,
> Butcher of thousands, threefold death be thine!
> So shall the English from thee gain relief,
> Scotland! be wise and choose a nobler chief.[7]

Edward would undoubtedly wish to be associated with these sentiments;
he gave expression to them, in legal terms, at the trial in 1305. That he was
paranoiac or had become so in the course of the war is also indisputable.
But he was a subtle man, as well as devious. It is possible that in his

treatment of Wallace there may lie a greater subtlety than that with which he has hitherto been credited. The surrender terms which Edward offered to the Scots in February 1304 were never open to Wallace. Edward was categorical: 'As for William Wallace, it is agreed, that he shall render himself up at the will and mercy of our sovereign lord the king as it shall seem good to him'.[8] There were others of the Scots, of course, who were not permitted to capitulate on the same conditions as Comyn: Wishart, James the Stewart, Fraser, and Soules were excluded. With time, however, they were to come into Edward's peace. Wallace could not. Edward repeated his theme of unconditional surrender in March in what appears to be a reply to a request for clarification from Alexander de Abernithyn: ' . . . and in reply to the matter wherein you have asked us to let you know whether it is our pleasure that you should hold out to William le Waleys any words of peace, know this, that it is not our pleasure by any means that either to him, or to any other of his company, you hold out any word of peace, unless they place themselves absolutely and in all things at our will, without any exception whatever'.[9] In the same letter Abernithyn is commended by Edward for his good work in keeping 'watch at the fords of Forth'. Here may be an indication that Wallace was in or expected to be in the vicinity. If so, he eluded the enemy, as he continued to do until August of the next year.

It is from material of this kind and from accounts of sporadic appearances by Wallace that we learn what little we know of his movements and activities between the surrender by Comyn and his capture by Menteith. He would be unable to rest for any length of time in any one place. If we can accept that he was given refuge by many unknown sympathisers, most drawn from the common people, we should not pretend that there were not Scots prepared to betray him into Edward's hands. This must have been especially true after the St. Andrews parliament of March 1304. There the peace terms were confirmed. Edward, in the cases of Simon Fraser, the garrison of Stirling, and Wallace, called for them to be outlawed by due process under Scots law and this was done. Again, as in the negotiations for the surrender in February and subsequently, the leaders of the Scots did not seek to divert Edward from his pursuit of Wallace. Both Fraser and the garrison of Stirling surrendered in July; Wallace alone remained.

The readiness with which the Scots consented to Edward's treatment of Wallace is cynical. It does, however, suggest that as early as the St. Andrews parliament they were being led by the English king towards the settlement of September 1305.[10] For Edward the capture and execution of Wallace were essential not simply on the grounds of removing the most stubborn of his opponents. The Scottish leaders acquiesced, by default at best, in the execution with its gruesome details. The suspicion that the death of Wallace satisfied them and Edward alike by its symbolism, the end of the old Scotland of resistance and the beginning of a new Scotland of full collaboration, cannot be overlooked. Edward brought the Scots, not unwillingly, in this direction in the months between February 1304 and August 1305.

Wallace stayed ahead of pursuit but with increasing difficulty. If we lack detail, it is obvious nonetheless that the pressure on him was intense. Edward's servants in 1303 had been futile or, more probably, frustrated by Wallace's knowledge of the terrain and the network of relatives and sympathisers on whom he could rely. His own experience of the raid and the ambush were to his advantage when they were employed against him. On 15 March 1303, for example, Edward had rewarded with money certain Scots who had been involved in an attempt to ambush him and Fraser.[11] In the autumn of that year, another equally unsuccessful attempt was made on the two. Reimbursement was made by Edward on 10 September to the pursuers for two horses killed in the skirmish from which Wallace and Fraser escaped[12] Wallace and Fraser were too wily to be taken easily. But it is evident that they cannot have survived without the help of many, unnamed Scots; the temptation to surrender the two outlaws must have been great but continued to be resisted by the majority.

Edward, with Wallace so elusive, had recourse in 1304 to what has been describing as the 'unattractive notion' of forcing former friends and associates to take part in the search for Wallace.[13] If unattractive, it was, for Edward, logical. He believed that he knew the Scots. Indeed he did but, for whatever reason, his blackmail, for such it was, did not result in the capture of Wallace. That at least is to the credit of the Scots; it may be impossible to clear them of accepting Wallace's death, but at least those on whom Edward tried his blackmail are not proven to have succumbed to it. We have the names of those whom Edward sought to coerce into the betrayal of Wallace. The return of James the Stewart, Sir Ingram de Umfraville, and Sir John Soules to the court and the favour of the king were not to be granted with letters of safe conduct until Wallace was taken.[14] Of the three Guardians Soules never came back to Scotland from France, while the others, each with his own code, do not stand accused of action against Wallace to secure the safe conducts. The lengths to which Edward would go can be more readily seen in another document.[15] In this he is more specific in the pressure he brings to bear: 'Sir Simon Fraser, Sir John Comyn , Sir Alexander Lindsay,[16] and Sir David Graham[17] are to exert themselves until twenty days after Christmas to capture William Wallace and hand him over to the king. And the king will take careful note of how each conducts himself, so that he may show most favour to the one who takes him with regard to mitigation of his sentence of exile or fine'.[18] Not content to exert pressure on the four, Edward was setting one against the other with the promise of a reward in the form of an easement of the penalties under which they already laboured.

Wallace himself, if on the run, was not entirely on the defensive. He was carrying on the war as best he could. We have seen evidence of his escapes from ambush. A much larger force threatened him in September 1304. This was led by Edward's trusted and able soldier, Aymer de Valence. In the company of some three hundred archers and with the banner of St. George to protect him, Valence met up with Wallace '. . . under Earnside'.[19] Wallace had not lost his skill. Although his own force could not equal that of Valence, he inflicted casualties on the mixed Anglo-Scottish troops and their horses and got away.[20] The English claimed that he had been put to flight, but that would count for little with the increasingly irate and demanding Edward. Such an encounter as this with Valence tested Wallace, and we have no way of knowing how close on this and other occasions he came to capture. But he was too astute not to leave himself a means of escape, the more so in the face of a large rather than a smaller force. For Wallace victory, in the circumstances, was escape. That is not to say that he was inevitably successful in this last year of his life. We do not know. He had been resoundingly defeated on at least one occasion in 1304, at the time of the negotiations for submission to Edward. From his winter quarters at Dunfermline Edward ordered a raid into the forest of Selkirk and areas of Lothian. It was a powerful force which he dispatched under the command of experienced soldiers, Segrave, Clifford, and Sir William Latimer. With them was Bruce. The intention was to lay hands on the Scottish leaders. In this it was unsuccessful, but there is no question that at Happrew, west of Peebles, Wallace and Fraser were defeated. Edward was less impressed by what the raid had achieved than by its failure to capture Wallace.[21]

There was one respect in which Wallace, as time ran away from him, had not changed. He struck at any with English sympathies or connections. This we can see from a document dated 24 March 1305 from Westminster; it is worthy of being reproduced in its entirety: 'To the helper, captain and justice of the water from the water of Forth to Orkeneye, or to him who supplies his place. The abbot of Redyng has besought the king to restore to him his island of May and the manner of Pednewen in that bailiwick, which were conferred upon the church of Redyng by former kings of Scotland and were delivered to the abbot as a cell of his church by the rebellion of John de Balliol, late king there, and which the abbot held peacefully as a cell of his church from the time of that delivery until William le Waleys and his accomplices, lately insurgents against the king in those parts, ejected the abbot and his men from the said island and manor; the king orders them to cause the abbot to have such seisin of the island and manor as he had before the commencement of the late war, and not to permit him to be disturbed by any one as to his seisin, so that after he has had seisin he may answer to everybody as he ought'.[22]

It is not merely in the reference to Wallace that the interest of the document lies. It is to be found more in the assumptions which are behind it and which find expression there. Scotland is Edward's; the war is over; Wallace has no army, only accomplices; he and they are insurgents. With none of this, of course, could Wallace agree. If technically the war could be said to be over with the submission of the Scots in February 1304, Wallace continued to set his face against any such acceptance. In his own mind, since he was Balliol's man and since Balliol alone was king of Scotland, there could be no question of insurgency, of rebellion. But it was not Wallace who wrote the documents or the law, and it was the law that he was an outlaw, to be hunted down, and, in Edward's view, a traitor. It mattered little now what Wallace thought, except that he was able to give brief expression to it at Westminster in August 1305. It mattered more what he did, and of that we have insufficient knowledge. We can only guess. The picture is one of desperate evasion, of emerging from one bolt-hole only to be driven into another by relentless English pressure, of hunger always and starvation sometimes, of unrecorded brushes with English and Scottish enemies, of the solace to be found in and with a few devoted friends careless of their own lives, of the comfort of religion, above all of that spirit peculiar to him which, somehow, sustained him to the end. Wallace cannot have hoped to escape – where was he to go? – but he would have hoped for a swift death, fighting sword in hand, as later, Blind Harry depicted him in so many adventures. That he was not to have.

It would be gratifying to be able to think that Wallace's continued defiance of Edward, even in the sordid circumstances in which he existed, stirred his people to further rebellion against Edward. But there was no such outcome. As he flitted from one hiding-place to another, Wallace, we may be sure, would speak to those he met with that same fierce commitment to the Scottish cause he had always had. Perhaps he gained adherents. But he could never again raise a force large enough to represent a genuine threat to the English. There is no dignity in suffering, and the Wallace who sought succour from the people from whom he had sprung must have been far from the man he once was. His words would carry conviction but now, in the last months of his life, he needed the nobles as he had not in 1297. They, if they had not forgotten him or found him an embarrassment as they made themselves amenable to Edward, had different values and priorities. These last months of Wallace's life have to be set against the background of Scottish indifference to the English occupation if not of active collaboration. With Wallace reduced to a fugitive and therefore, in practical terms, impotent, where was the leadership to come from? Comyn and Bruce, in an alliance of whom most hope of a national revival lay, could not work together. It is true that when Wallace was captured, Bruce was no more than six months away from the murder of Comyn and the subsequent seizure of the throne of Scotland. At the time of the execution, no one could possibly foresee such a sequence of events. The 'band' into which Bruce had entered with Lamberton on 11 July 1304 has been interpreted as evidence that the security in which Edward believed he held Scotland was deceptive.[23] But if this was so, more than a year after the band, at the time of Wallace's death, Bruce had risked nothing and, like Comyn, of whose motives and intentions we know even less, had not been inspired by Wallace's resistance to the point of emulating him. No doubt there were whispers of abhorrence for Edward and his policies; these would be the staple of Scottish conversation. No doubt some among the Scots leaders, as they prepared for Edward's parliament of September 1305, were genuinely shocked by the horror of Edward's treatment of Wallace. But there was no more than that. Neither his last resistance nor his execution roused his countrymen.

The end for Wallace came suddenly. He was captured in or near Glasgow on 3 August. His capture fell to Sir John Menteith. As a subject of Edward, Menteith had no reason to think of Wallace as other than an enemy and his capture as an honour. From an early date, however, the belief grew that Wallace had been taken by treachery, and it is upon Menteith that the odium has fallen. Blind Harry did not spare him,[24] and Menteith's reputation never recovered from the criticism. Not satisfied with making Menteith an English sympathiser, in itself crime enough, Harry has him betray the closest of friends in Wallace, godfather to his children. To treachery therefore was added betrayal of a friend for money. Recent commentators, however, while they can never hope to rehabilitate Menteith in the popular mind, have sought to excuse him if not to exonerate him. As will be argued,[25] contemporary opinion may very well have understood Menteith's conduct. Originally a firm supporter of the Scottish cause, Menteith, son of that Walter Stewart who had held the earldom of Menteith by right of his wife,[26] had come into Edward's peace at an unknown date. It may have been between September 1303 and March 1304.[27] Like so many Scots, Bruce and Comyn not excepted, Menteith had no apparent difficulty in changing from one side to the other. His was the fervour of the convert. He was rewarded for his defection to the English cause by Edward who made him sheriff of Dumbarton and keeper of its castle. It was natural that having given his oath to Edward, he should, again like others among his contrymen, see no shame in participation in the pursuit and capture of Wallace. If Menteith was guilty of treachery, it is impossible to believe that, given the opportunity which fell to him, others would not have acted in the same manner.

What Wallace was doing in Glasgow we do not know. He was, apparently, alone, although one English chronicler would have us believe otherwise. It is Peter of Langtoft who regales us with this story: 'We have heard news among companions of William Wallace, the master of the thieves; Sir John de Menteith followed him close at his heels; and took him in bed beside his strumpet'.[28] When taken, alone or not, he had in his possession documents, since lost, which might have explained his presence there. The possibility that they implicated certain Scots with him may be doubted. Their seizure, as far as we can tell, led to no arrests. Edward, although he had good reason to think the Scottish question settled, was suspicious by now of all about him. He would not have hesitated to act if the papers in Wallace's possession had given him cause. Wallace may have been in Glasgow in the hope of taking ship; if so, he can hardly be blamed for seeking a respite abroad from the intolerable strain of the pursuit. His presence there could have been in search of allies for yet another strike at the English. Whatever his reasons, they have not come down to us.

As we are ignorant of his reasons for being in Glasgow, the circumstances surrounding his capture are, equally, uncertain. English accounts stress that he was taken by his own countrymen. We need not be surprised by this; true or not, the belief that they had betrayed him to Edward isolated him still further from what the English claimed was Scottish acceptance of their rule. A particular Scot is named in connection with the capture of Wallace. This is Ralph de Haliburton. He came from a family close to Wallace at the beginning of his adventures in 1297. Ralph de Haliburton himself was a member of the garrison of Stirling Castle under Sir William Oliphant and upon its fall in July 1304 was sent into imprisonment in England. On 28 February 1305 he was released on condition that he helped to capture Wallace.[29] He was released into the custody of a Scottish knight, Sir John Mowbray, who became responsible for him. Mowbray, himself taken a prisoner to England after the battle of Dunbar, was yet another Scot who changed sides. Whatever his precise part in the capture of Wallace, Mowbray, unlike Menteith, has escaped criticism, as indeed has Haliburton for whom he was responsible. What exactly the released Haliburton did to ensure Wallace's capture or whether he was, as has been suggested, Wallace's supposed servant, the mysterious Jack Short, we have no means of knowing. It is tempting in the search for an answer to revert to the traditional account, that treachery was indeed how Wallace was taken. Blind Barry has him allowing himself to be bound by Menteith on the incredible excuse that in this way Menteith would be able to smuggle him, supposedly already a prisoner, through the English lines.[30] That Wallace, for so long a master of self-preservation, should be so deceived is both ludicrous and insulting to his memory. He was captured either through a well-laid trap – for an escape along the Clyde was a possibility of which the English would not be ignorant – or his presence was reported to Menteith who carried out his duty for which he was rewarded with land by the English king.

Wallace was at once sent south. There is no record of an attempt at rescue, although his capture cannot have gone unremarked. He was transferred into the custody of Sir John Segrave for the crossing into England. His fate was already decided, as he must have known, but it is unlikely that he could have suspected that Edward intended to give him the formality of a trial and even more unlikely that he could have suspected its purpose.

NOTES

1. Matthew of Westminster: *Flores Historiarum*, ii, 118.
2. Barrow: *Robert Bruce*, 181; McNair Scott, 64.
3. Chap. 4, above.
4. *Cal. Docs. Scot.*, iii, 425-7.
5. *Flores Hist.* ii, 319-20.
6. Chap. 10 below.
7. Maxwell trans., 176.
8. *Cal. Docs. Scot.*, ii, 1444-5 and 1463.
9. *Ibid.*, 1463.
10. For a different view of the situation between Edward and the Scottish nobles see Barrow: *Robert Bruce*, 187-9.
11. *D.N.B.*, 569.
12. *Ibid.*
13. Kightly, 185.
14. *Cal. Docs. Scot.*, ii, 1563.
15. Palgrave: *Docs.*, 276.
16. Later a supporter of Robert I in 1306.
17. It will be remembered that it was Graham who played a leading role in the fracas at

Peebles in August 1299. He it was who laid claim to Wallace's lands, thus setting in train the quarrel between the Scottish leaders. See chap. 7 above.

18. Whether any of them inclined to carry out Edward's wishes we do not know for certain. None of them took part in the actual capture; for that reason, if for no other, they must be exonerated.

19. *Cal. Docs. Scot.*, iv, 477.

20. *Ibid.*

21. *Cal. Docs. Scot.*, ii, 1432.

22. *Cal. Close Rolls*, 24 March 1305, Westminster.

23. Barrow: *Robert Bruce*, 184-5.

24. Eleventh book.

25. Kightly, 186; Barrow: *Robert Bruce*, 193.

26. He was still engaged on the Scottish side in September 1303: Stevenson *Docs. Illust. Hist. Scot.*, ii, 453. He was Edward's man at the latest by March of the next year. *Cal. Docs. Scot.*, ii, 1474. His reward for the capture of Wallace, generally given as £100 of land, is found in Stevenson: *Wall. Docs.*, 101-2 147.

27. He was keeper of the castle of Dumbarton.

28. The failure of other chroniclers to use this story is indicative. Wright (ed.): *Peter of Langtoft: Metrical Chronicle.*

29. We are left to guess why he was considered especially likely to accomplish the task. With him as with others in the story of Wallace's capture, it is not easy to understand how Wallace came to trust him or them after so many years of pursuit.

30. Eleventh book.

CHAPTER 10

The Time of Glory, 1305

Wallace reached London on Sunday, 22 August, and was led through streets filled with jeering, abusive citizens to the property of one William de Leyre, an alderman and former sheriff, in the parish òf Fenchurch, where he spent the night. Early the next morning he was brought on horseback to Westminster Hall through streets thronged once more. He formed part of a procession, directed by Segrave and his brother Geoffrey, which included those named by Edward to sit in judgement on him, as well as sheriffs and aldermen of the city. Inside the hall, at the south end, a scaffold had been erected, and there Wallace was made to stand. On his head his captors had placed a crown of laurel, to mock him, it was said, for his boast that one day he would wear a crown in this place.[1] It is unlikely that Wallace would ever make such a remark. Neither before Stirling nor Falkirk did he act the braggart, although he was not above the use of a title when he felt it justified.[2] The placing of a crown on his head was part of a deliberate policy of humiliation. The practice was not unique. In the following year, his old ally and companion, Simon Fraser, in London to suffer the same fate as Wallace, was crowned with a garland of periwinkle.[3]

The commission which Edward had empowered to deal with Wallace was a formidable one.[4] The principal legal figure was Peter Mallore or Mallory, justiciar of England, whose name is frequently found in the records of the period. He was especially active in 1306 in the aftermath of Bruce's seizure of the crown of Scotland. Mallore condemned, among others, Christopher Seton, who had seconded Bruce in the murder of Comyn and had himself cut down Comyn's uncle; Alexander Scrymgeour, standard-bearer of Scotland and an associate of Wallace when the latter was Guardian, and John Strathbogie earl of Atholl, the first of his station to be executed for treason since Waltheof was beheaded by order of William I in 1086. With Mallore sat another judge, Ralph de Sandwych, a man of vast experience under Edward and his predecessor. He would later sentence Simon Fraser to death. As constable of the Tower of London he had been responsible for the custody of some notable figures of the war with Scotland, among them the earls of Menteith, Ross, and Atholl, after the battle of Dunbar. The mayor of London, John le Blunt, represented the city, while a fourth member of the commission was John de Bacwell, who would meet a melancholy end, suffocated to death at the coronation of Edward II in February 1308. Finally, there was Segrave. Of those who faced Wallace on that day only Segrave, a soldier, would be sure of his respect. A veteran of the Welsh wars, Segrave subsequently had a distinguished career against the Scots. He fought at Falkirk and was present at the siege of Caerlaverock in 1303 and of Stirling in 1304. He was wounded and captured by Fraser at Roslin in February 1303 but later rescued. In early 1304 he inflicted a defeat on Wallace, then in the company of Fraser, not far from Peebles. Thereafter, on Edward's instructions, he devoted his energies to the capture of Wallace. As we shall see, he was not free of Wallace even after the execution.

Two factors have served to obscure the nature of the proceedings in Westminster Hall. The first is the undoubted horror of the sentence on Wallace, the second the charge of treason laid against him. To concentrate on these is to misunderstand Edward's intention. He meant to destroy Wallace in body and in reputation and to that end brought him to trial as an outlaw as well as a traitor. In that context, the sentence was in accordance with the law as it stood not merely in England but in Scotland. Edward was a master in the use and abuse of the law. This characteristic had been noted long before at the time of the rebellion of Simon de Montfort when as Prince Edward he had prompted this comment on his behaviour: 'The treachery or falseness by which he gains his ends he calls prudence; the way he arrives at his object, be it ever so crooked, is reputed to be straight; when wrong serves his ambition it is called right; he calls lawful whatever he wills, and thinks himself above the law'.[5] Wallace was now to discover the truth of this. For Edward the form was important if the outcome was itself already decided.

To speak of a trial in modern terms is inaccurate. Wallace was permitted no jury. No witnesses were called. There was no plea. Wallace was given no opportunity to defend himself, although he did succeed in making one interruption. Mallore read the indictment and Segrave the sentence. There was no appeal. Wallace was immediately led to execution. While shocking to us, the whole procedure was in keeping with contemporary practice.[6] It is crucial to an understanding of the treatment of Wallace to remember that Wallace had been outlawed at the St. Andrews parliament in the previous year and, in all probability, at least once prior to that. Nor should it be overlooked that the outlawing of Wallace had been by due Scottish process in 1304. An outlaw, once proclaimed, had no entitlement even to the formality of a trial. His life was forfeit, and the hand of every man was turned against him. If the law was in a sense admitting its inability to deal with the criminal, it was at the same time, as in the case of Wallace, making his crimes manifest to the public and thus making summary justice possible. If taken, therefore, the outlaw could expect only that judgement would be carried out against him with or without the formality of a trial. The status of a man did not protect him from this harsh aspect of outlawry. In the reign of Edward II, his cousin Thomas earl of Lancaster was outlawed with various of his confederates. When he fell into Edward's hands, Lancaster was at once convicted and executed.[7] In respect of the summary, not to say sham, nature of the proceedings in Westminster Hall, Wallace was treated no worse than any other outlaw.

Edward was, however, careful to emphasise that the decision to outlaw Wallace had followed upon a refusal of clemency. Wallace was shown to be not merely an outlaw but an obdurate one. There is a clear indication of this in the indictment.[8] The reference was to events after Falkirk. It would be easy to dismiss this offer as a formality and its appearance in the indictment as evidence of Edward's hypocrisy. We should not too readily assume this. The offer may mark a stage in Edward's approach to the problem of Wallace which has not perhaps received adequate attention. He had not always vindictively sought Wallace's death. His decision not to accept custody of Wallace from Philip of France has already been touched on.[9] It was a peculiar episode for which we have no explanation, but it does suggest that at the time Edward saw little threat in Wallace and no need to put him to death then. Edward's behaviour towards Bruce and other Scottish leaders demonstrates tht he sought an accommodation until he felt himself utterly betrayed. Once he had reached that point, he became demonic in pursuit of those who had spurned him. This was so in the case of Wallace. It was not until February 1304 that Edward took the ultimate step of refusing to Wallace that clemency which he had just held out to the other Scots. From there it was, in legal process, but a step to St. Andrews and thence to Westminster Hall.

The list of crimes with which Wallace the outlaw was charged by Mallore was an impressive one.[10] It included killings, arson, destruction of property, and sacrilege. These crimes relate mostly to the period between the start of his rebellion against English rule and the close of his invasion of the north of England. Then, indeed, he had burned villages, towns and religious establishments and, Mallore stated, spared neither the young nor the old, nuns nor priests. None of this Wallace could deny. This part of the indictment illustrates how well he had carried out his intention to wage war against the English. The more undisciplined of his followers committed atrocities in England which stain his name, but their savagery was the currency of war at the time. He had too as a matter of policy attacked the representatives of the English Church which for him threatened the Scottish cause. All of these crimes constituted a standard accusation, one which might with equal truth been made against Edward himself. Wallace was after all repaying like with like. The accusation was designed to prove that Wallace's crimes were common knowledge or notorious in the public mind and therefore beyond doubt or defence. Once more, in this, Edward was calling upon precedent. In 1287 he had had the Welshman, Rhys ap Maredudd, declared a notorious criminal. Wallace, a public outlaw, was cited for crimes which were of themselves public knowledge.

The one specific charge against Wallace in this section of the indictment was the murder of Hazelrig. The motives behind the murder have been a source of debate but not the deed itself.[11] Had it been the sole crime laid against Wallace, it would have been sufficient to bring the death penalty – by hanging – in a Scottish as well as in an English court. The symbolic importance of the murder may however have led Edward to include it at Westminster. With the murder Wallace had emerged as a leader of the resistance; the blow to English prestige must therefore be avenged.

The outlawry and the murder were of themselves overwhelming. The case based on them was irrefutable, and for each there was an accepted penalty. When, however, we turn to the question of treason, Edward's argument is less secure. It was the charge of treason which brought from Wallace his only recorded contribution to the proceedings. He denied – we may safely assume that he did so with the utmost vehemence – that he was a traitor. He had never sworn allegiance to Edward. That we know to be a fact. Where the likes of Bruce and Comyn, and even Fraser, had given their allegiance, and their service, to the English king, and at various times throughout the war, Wallace had resolutely refused to do so. He might have saved his life by emulating these lords. He remained Balliol's man. Edward was not deterred by this.

It is difficult for us to comprehend how, if Wallace had never given his allegiance to Edward, the king could accuse him of treason. In a crucial sense, however, the definition of treason was the prerogative of the monarch. Edward had recourse in the case of Wallace to conviction on the king's record, a development in the law of treason which was of his own devising. It allowed him to bring Wallace before the court, to have the accusation rehearsed, and to secure the verdict he sought. He needed only to present his statement of the crimes with which he charged the prisoner; the judgement he demanded followed without delay or debate. The abuse possible under this system was to lead to public disquiet. It was the treason trials engineered by Edward II which, however, demonstrated the extent of that abuse. Appeals at the start of the reign of Edward III, for example those against the judgements in the cases of Thomas of Lancaster and Andrew de Harcla, prompted discussion. When parliament at length turned to Edward III for a definition of treason, he produced it in 1352; it is that statute which is still the basis of English law on the subject. But Wallace was, in 1305, quite literally dependent upon his enemy for the definition of treason as it applied to him.

What was that definition? Edward was, as always, careful to state it in some detail. He returned first to the surrender to him by Balliol of the kingdom of Scotland in 1296. This act, he argued, made the inhabitants of that country, whether or not they accepted Balliol's surrender and Edward's consequent sovereignty, subjects of the English king. To him Scotsmen of all degrees had at that time and afterwards sworn their loyalty. No Scot was in Edward's view excused from that loyalty by the mere fact of not having sworn it. It is a wholly unacceptable argument to our way of thinking; our sympathies cannot but lie with Wallace.

The immediate question of allegiance thus settled to Edward's own satisfaction, the indictment as it deals with treason encompasses Wallace's rebellion, his assumption of the title of Guardian of Scotland, his convening of parliaments, and his seduction of the people of Scotland into seeking an alliance with France, at the time England's enemy. All these acts were hostile to Edward and by that token treasonable. Their inclusion in the indictment, as with the evidence relating to the waging of war, tells us of the impact made by Wallace in his struggle for the independence of Scotland. If he was a soldier, he was no less a statesman. In his anxiety to blacken Wallace's name, Edward was in the event providing the proof of his captive's achievements. There is one, and to us intriguing, addition to the recital of treasonable acts given by Mallore. Wallace had displayed banners while in the field against the English. This was a charge frequently found in treason trials of this and other periods. It was raised in 1318 with Gilbert de Middleton and against Thomas of Lancaster and certain of his associates after the battle of Boroughbridge in 1322. As late as 1497, in the reign of Henry VII, Lord Audley faced a similar charge. To display one's banners while in arms was held to be a declaration of war against the monarch who was alone capable of instigating a just and legal war.[12] The court chose once more to ignore that Wallace had never been Edward's man.

It will be seen that Edward had produced a damning indictment against Wallace for treason as he did for outlawry. The case proven to the satisfaction of the court, Segrave read the sentence, which was implemented without delay. For his treasons Wallace was drawn, tied to a hurdle – perhaps as in the case of Fraser,[13] wrapped in an ox-hide – at the tails of horses to the place of execution. To be drawn was recognised as the mark of a traitor. Edward did not devise this aspect of the punishment for Wallace, nor had it originated in the war with Scotland. Ten years previously, Sir Thomas Turberville, guilty of spying for France, was drawn, as had been David ap Gruffyd in 1283. The use of the hurdle or the hide served to protect the victim and save him for the viler aspects of the sentence; he might otherwise have been ripped apart on the surfaces over which he was pulled. Wallace's route to his torment at Smithfield took him from Westminster past the Tower, to Aldgate, and onwards by a circuitous route through the city for more than four miles, to the delight of the populace.

At Smithfield, for the murders, robberies, and other felonies he had committed both in his own country and in England, he was hanged, as standard a punishment as drawing was for treason. He was cut down while still alive so that he might be spared none of the bestialities ahead. He was disembowelled and in all probability emasculated, although the official record makes no mention of this. Matthew of Westminster relates that Wallace was 'mutilated', a clear reference to what was commonly inflicted on traitors.[14] For his sacrilege, the burning of religious establishments and relics, his heart, liver, lungs, and entrails were cast upon a fire. From these, it was believed, issued the thoughts which led him to sacrilege. That disembowelling and the burning of entrails was a fitting punishment for sacrilege was well established; it appears to have been first used in the case of David ap Gruffyd. Not even his royal blood had saved him from this particularly revolting aspect of the judgement. Wallace was decapitated for his outlawry. Strangely, decapitation of itself was considered a not dishonourable death, used throughout the centuries for nobles convicted of treason or other crimes. Waltheof had died thus, as did Lancaster.

But Edward was not finished with Wallace, even now. His head was placed on a pole on London Bridge, no doubt that those who passed that way might marvel at Edward's justice. His body was hacked into four pieces. One quarter was sent to Newcastle upon Tyne and there exhibited above the common sewer, to the delight of those who recalled Wallace's brutal invasion of the district in 1297-1298. A second part went to Berwick, that town of so great and tragic a significance in the war which had made his name and brought about his death. A third part was hung at Perth, the town of St. John, of such strategic value to Scots and English alike, where, according to Blind Harry, Wallace performed some of his most spectacular deeds. There is some dispute as to the destination of the fourth part. Lanercost differs from the official version in giving Aberdeen for Stirling. Both towns were familiar to Wallace. The former had witnessed one of the more calculatedly brutal episodes associated with him: the hanging of a number of Scots who had defied him. Stirling was the scene of his great victory. For that reason it may be the likelier choice, in keeping with Edward's intention to blacken Wallace's memory. It was Segrave who was commanded to see to the transportation of Wallace's quarters to their destinations. For this he was paid fifteen shillings.[15]

Thus Wallace perished, horribly if memorably. Edward had removed his most persistent but not, as time would show, his most dangerous enemy. In doing so, as time would also show, he had made a colossal blunder. It became, and remained, an article of faith in Scotland that Wallace had died a hero and a martyr. Hero he undoubtedly was, by any measure. From the moment of his appearance at Lanark, he was a hero in personal, military, and political terms, brief though his supremacy was. And Edward, although he did not live to learn this, had made him into a martyr on 23 August 1305. Blind Harry tells us that by his death at the hands of the English Wallace entered into 'lasting bliss'.[16] He had entered into glory, his eyes fixed, Harry says, on his most beloved possession, his psalter, held before him by Clifford.[17] And it was into a kind of glory that Wallace indeed had gone. His name survives in the popular memory, where that of others, with a crucial or melancholy role in the War of Independence, has not. The name of Simon Fraser means little today. Yet he served the Scottish cause well, fought with Wallace, did not betray him when it might have been to his own advantage, joined Bruce in 1306, and met the same ghastly end as Wallace. Alexander Bruce, brother of Robert, was executed at Carlisle by Edward. Dean of Glasgow, Alexander had been known at Cambridge for his scholarship and his character. He too fought for the cause, although incompetently, and fell before Edward's violent and uncertain temper. But who speaks now of Alexander Bruce? Christopher Seton, husband of Christina Bruce, perished at Dumfries, where he had helped in the murder of Comyn. Seton is forgotten. Like his brother, John Wallace was taken to London and there put to death. Not even his relationship with William has saved John Wallace from anonymity. Not one of these, or any of the long list of Edward's victims, not even one of the standing of the earl of Atholl, has as lasting a fame or as firm a hold on the imagination of the people of Scotland as William Wallace.

What cannot easily be demonstrated is when Wallace's reputation, the one he has come to enjoy, was first established in Scotland. The indictment presented on Edward's behalf at Westminster Hall would appear to suggest that he meant not only to destroy Wallace's body – which was his to dispose of – but his reputation. That he failed to do the latter in the long term has perhaps led us to overlook the possibility that in the short term he did succeed in his aim. Wallace had been stigmatised as an outlaw and a traitor. It is difficult to argue that the verdict would have been radically different in a Scottish court, whether dominated or not by Edward, had the charges been those used at Westminster. There was a frightening unanimity in both countries on the subject of the outlaw and the traitor. Nor would the sentence have differed. For confirmation we may look to the Scone or 'Black' parliament of August 1320. There the members of the so-called 'Soules conspiracy' were brought to justice. On that occasion Robert Bruce did not scruple to use the full severity of the law if he thought it warranted. It is true that unlike Edward he did temper justice with mercy in certain of the sentences.[18] But a famous figure of the period, Ingram de Umfraville, was so disturbed by Bruce's execution of David Brechin – both the judgement itself and the manner of punishment – that he withdrew his allegiance to Bruce and returned to his estates in England. All this took place when Scotland was secure from the English menace. Not even as humane a king as Bruce could entirely escape from his own temper and the cruelty into which it led him.

What then was the reaction in Scotland to the death of Wallace? It is here that we are perhaps most unfortunate in our lack of contemporary Scottish evidence on which to draw. We do know that the death of Wallace did not prevent the Scottish lords from advising Edward on and in some cases participating in the new form of government for Scotland which emerged from the parliament of Westminster in September 1305. While it is correct that discussions on the new council for Scotland had been taking place before the capture and death of Wallace, it is equally correct that, one month after his execution, men with whom he had fought were prepared to assist Edward's lieutenant in Scotland, John of Brittany. Not even Bruce can be entirely cleared of this association, despite at least one strenuous defence of him.[19] It would be comforting to draw a connection between Wallace's death and Bruce's rebellion of 1306, but it would be to fly in the face of reason. Bruce had long aspired to the throne and had been plotting to achieve his aim, whether or not with the help of Wallace we cannot tell.[20] But whatever the motive behind the murder of Comyn – whether Bruce feared betrayal by Comyn or was thwarted by him in his plans – it was a rash and unconsidered act. It tells us that, when provoked or baulked, Bruce possessed the more extreme reactions of his grandfather, the Competitor, rather than the more equable temperament of his father, the earl of Carrick. Bruce's subsequent moves, which involved him in rebellion against Edward, were the consequence of the murder; he was not driven by any desire to avenge Wallace.

Bruce's whole relationship with Wallace was a strange one,[21] but it may well be that the clue to the question of Wallace's reputation is to be found in certain of Bruce's actions once he became king. It must be remembered that prior to the murder of Comyn, Bruce's behaviour had always been dictated by a degree of self-interest absent in Wallace. His family had always stressed the strength and legitimacy of its claim to the throne. Bruce himself fought for years to establish that legitimacy against the claims of Edward II. It might not serve his purpose in this struggle to have his name linked with that of Wallace, a convicted traitor and outlaw. This question of legitimacy may explain the otherwise surprising omission of Wallace's name from Barbour's account of Bruce. Even in the famous speech which he puts into his hero's mouth at Bannockburn Barbour can find no place for a mention of Wallace. Uplifting though Bruce's address is, noble as its sentiments are, he does not in Barbour's report call upon the name of Wallace to inspire his army. It may not be irrelevant that after the completion of his work Barbour received first a gift of money and then a pension from Robert II. There was again war with England. Barbour would thus fulfil the role Blind Harry gave himself at the time of James III if with different motives: to produce a story which would stir and unite a people governed by a weak king in the face of the enemy. If this argument is correct, it makes Barbour's treatment of Wallace the more striking.

More significant, however, because of the firm evidence, is Bruce's attitude to Menteith, the traditional villain in the story of Wallace's capture. It was noted earlier[22] that Menteith, in seizing Wallace, was acting on the instructions of Edward, to whom he was bound by his oath of loyalty. It is entirely possible that Comyn, Lindsay, or Graham might have played Menteith's role had opportunity offered. But that opportunity, and with it the loathing of posterity, fell to Menteith. If in the capture of Wallace Menteith had been acting by reason of his oath to Edward, he was not averse to an attempt to lay hands upon the possessions of those who had joined Bruce in 1306.[23] Yet, in 1309, Bruce accepted Menteith into his peace and bestowed lands upon him. Menteith's name, further, was one of those associated with the Declaration of Arbroath. Menteith, first for the Scottish cause, then Edward's man, and finally a supporter of Bruce, did not suffer in the latter's eyes because he had handed Wallace over to the English any more than he did by his shifts of allegiance. If four years after Wallace's death Menteith was received by Bruce and was subsequently so to be established that he was involved in the Declaration of Arbroath, we are entitled to wonder whether it was Wallace's reputation rather than that of Menteith which had suffered in those years.

If this is indeed the case, it may explain, along with Barbour's omission of Wallace from his tale, the reticence of his contemporary, Fordun, on the matter of the inspirational nature of Wallace's reputation. If Fordun tells us how Wallace learned of the meaning of freedom and casts Menteith as the villain who betrayed Wallace to the English who tore the hero apart in London, we have to wait for Andrew Wyntoun for the quintessential and lasting Scottish view of Wallace:

> In all England there was not then
> As William Wallace so true a man.
> Whatever he did against their nation
> They made him ample provocation
> Nor to them sworn never was he
> To fellowship, faith or loyalty.[24]

Wyntoun's description of Wallace, embroidered by Blind Harry, has prevailed. The English account of Wallace is ignored. Yet neither is wholly satisfactory. Only by utilising both sources, together with such documentary evidence as we possess, can we hope to achieve an understanding of this remarkable man.

NOTES

1. Stevenson (ed.): *Documents Illustrative of Sir William Wallace*, 189.

2. Walter of Hemingford: *Chronicon*, 142. Wallace summoned Carlisle to surrender under the title of 'the Conqueror'. Given his recent victory and his almost unimpeded progress through the north of England, however, the title may be said to be not undeserved.

3. Wright (ed.): *Political Songs of England*, 218.

4. *Calendar of the Patent Rolls*, 18 August 1305. Stubbs (ed.): *Chronicles of the Reigns of Edward I and Edward II*, i. 139, includes Geoffrey de Segrave among the judges.

5. Wright, *op. cit.*, 94, in 'the Battle of Lewes'.

6. For a contemporary account of the trial, see Stubbs (ed.): *Chronicles*, i. 139-142. Modern commentaries appear in Bellamy: *The Law of Treason in England in the Later Middle Ages*, 34 *et seq.* and Keen: 'Treason Trials under the Law of Arms' (*E.H.R.*), *passim*.

7. Brie (ed.): *The Brut*, i, 222.

8. Mallore read: '. . . and offered you mercy if you surrendered, you did despise his offer, and were outlawed in his court as a thief and a felon according to the law of England and Scotland . . . '

9. See chap. 7.

10. The indictment is printed in Stubbs (ed.): *Chronicles*, i, pp. 139-142.

11. Henry the Minstrel (Blind Harry): *Schir William Wallace*, sixth book, gives the traditional story. Kightly: *Folk Heroes of Britain*, chap. 6, is the most recent summary of the accounts.

12. See on this Bellamy and Keen. Also Keen: *The Laws of War in the Later Middle Ages*, 105 *et seq.*

13. Wright, *op. cit.*, 220.

14. Matthew of Westminster: *Flores Historiarum*, iii, 123-4.

15. *Calendar of the Patent Rolls*, 29 September 1305.

16. Eleventh book, 1406.

17. Eleventh book, 1397-8.

18. Barrow: *Robert Bruce*, 429-30.

19. Barron: *The Scottish War of Independence*, chap. 15.

20. The documents found on Wallace at the time of his capture, had they survived, might have answered the question.

21. It is returned to in the Conclusion.

22. Chapter 9.

23. Barrow, *op. cit.*, 448.

24. Wyntoun: *Oryginale Cronykil of Scotland*.

Conclusion

If William Wallace unquestionably died a hero and a martyr in London on 23 August 1305, he also died a failure. That is a harsh judgement, but a realistic one if we measure what he accomplished in practical terms against the task which he had set himself after the murder of Heselrig at Lanark in May 1297. That is the proper, indeed the only, date at which to begin the study of Wallace. We have to confess our ignorance of him before then. What information we can assemble about his family, what tradition and supposition have made of him, what we have come to believe of him, none of this gives us an accurate picture of him before the murder. The motives behind the murder itself are likewise hidden from us. Whether he killed Heselrig as the representative of a hated regime or as an act of revenge is immaterial; its significance lies in the impact it made upon contemporary opinion. We can see in Wallace's actions after Lanark a pattern which allows us to argue with more certainty about his intentions even if we are, again, ignorant of much of his life.

To rid his country of the English and to see it sovereign, with its own king, these were the twin ambitions of Wallace's life after Lanark. He achieved neither. At the time of Wallace's death Edward I was master of Scotland and about to promulgate, in the forthcoming parliament of Westminster, that Ordinance whereby Scotland, no longer conceded the status of a 'realm' but described merely as a 'land', was to be governed. That strange and elusive man, John Balliol, for whom Wallace had fought to the death, had not been restored to the throne which he had lost, perhaps to his own relief, nine years previously. Scotland had reverted in 1305 to its condition in 1296, before Wallace's first recorded appearance in the war with England. It was an occupied and defeated country, its people repressed, its affairs in the hands of a foreign monarch. When, many years after Wallace's death, Scotland was finally free and with its own king, that was the work of a man with whom his relationship had been at best an uneasy one. We do well to remember, if we are to understand Wallace, that had he escaped Edward I and lived to witness an independent Scotland, it would have been as an opponent of Bruce, if not as a proclaimed traitor to him. Balliol's man, Wallace would not have changed his allegiance.

The fact that Wallace died alone is too readily forgotten. He was butchered as a punishment and as a spectacle for the populace of London and for those Scots present in the capital in anticipation of the parliament. To them and to the English sympathisers still in Scotland, he was a rebel and a traitor. They had condemned him as such at the St. Andrews parliament in March of the preceding year. There is no evidence to suggest that they had changed their minds about him in the period leading up to his capture and trial. We need not charge Bruce, Comyn, Lamberton and the others with complicity in Wallace's end. They viewed it with apparent indifference, the indifference of the collaborator. It is an ugly and emotive word, but unavoidable. Wallace had become an embarrassment to them. He represented the old, stern Scotland, that of resistance. Edward had offered them a new Scotland, that of collaboration, and they had accepted it. Bruce, Comyn, and Lamberton, all three like Wallace Guardians, were nominated to occupy important positions in the government which Edward had established for Scotland. They were not the only Scots for whom he found a place. It is idle to speculate about the thoughts of these men, whether they whispered against the sentence on Wallace, whether they planned rebellion or not at some stage in the future. We can only judge them by their actions. They collaborated with Edward in the dispositions he was making for Scotland. Wallace's execution, for them as for Edward, was a symbolic prelude. It marked a beginning.

It was both Wallace's strength and his weakness that he had refused to model himself on those who denied him in 1305. Because he would not bend, he was seen in a period of upheaval as capable of assuming leadership and with it the burden of government. If he benefited from the opportunity which circumstances presented, he showed himself, once installed in authority, a man of exceptional qualities. His success both before and during his Guardianship has been taken for granted. That is unjust. We have to bear in mind that it was not only his rise which was without parallel in the war. Equally remarkable, surely, was his decision to challenge, and then to overcome, the obstacles which he faced because of his origins. We do not know whether Wallace was a modest man; that he was determined is self-evident. One more open to suggestion might have flinched when in 1297 he saw opening before him a future wholly different from that for which he had been raised. He could have pleaded unfitness and he would have been believed by men whose prejudices excluded him from their councils. By stepping forward he committed a revolutionary act. He was at once isolated from his origins and from his feudal superiors.

His weakness was that by his unwillingness to learn the skills of those same superiors he could not hope to survive in the only conditions henceforth open to him. The charge in the indictment of August 1305 that Edward had offered him clemency after Falkirk only to have it refused by

Wallace is difficult to refute for two reasons. Firstly, the refusal itself is typical of Wallace; he did not know how to compromise in the struggle with the English king. Secondly, Edward had won at Falkirk a victory which, based on the precedent of Dunbar, appeared to be conclusive. A staggering number of Scots had been slaughtered with a minimum of English casualties. Edward no doubt knew of the defection or treachery of the Scottish lords. He would assume, as did the Scottish lords themselves, that defeat had ended Wallace's period of supremacy. Edward thus had every reason to believe that resistance was broken. Wallace, knighted and holder of the honourable title of Guardian of Scotland, was worthy of terms. They would not have been severe; Edward was aware of the value of magnanimity. He had misjudged his man. After Dunbar, the Scots had crumbled, disgracefully. Under Wallace they were of another calibre. Wallace's refusal of clemency was a clear indication to Edward, as was Stirling, that with him the character of the war had changed. Wallace had reached the level of his superiors through his own efforts but he was never able to adopt their standards; it was a fatal stance.

Wallace taught the Scots, after Lanark, that resistance to the English was possible under a regime which did not depend on those who by birth and inheritance laid claim to its leadership. In him ability rose above station. He set an example which was not merely novel but dangerous. He threatened to upset that social balance to which the Scottish nobility, like Edward himself, subscribed. For this reason he was suspect. Not even his selfless rejection of ultimate power for himself, both when he was sole Guardian and in the chaotic aftermath of Falkirk, could prove to the lords that he scorned that ambition which they took for granted in themselves. It is difficult to see who could have prevented him from seizing power while Guardian had he wanted. He would have served himself, but not the cause to which he was dedicated had he chosen to do so. His refusal was a gift to his country.

Success at Stirling was followed by defeat at Falkirk, and it is that defeat which has dominated criticism of Wallace the soldier. If understandable, that is unfair. Wallace was not a trained soldier and, as far as we know, had had no experience of warfare before 1297. After Lanark, he inherited an army of a size he could never have contemplated or wanted. To him came the men who had met with defeat at Dunbar and, worse, those who had not fought but were drawn to him now as the bearer of hope. That was no foundation on which to build. Yet, first at Stirling, then at Falkirk, he showed himself masterly in the deployment and handling of large masses of infantry. At the former, with the opportunity given him by the incompetence of Surrey and the recklessness of Cressingham, he so gauged the moment to release his infantry as to ensure victory. At Falkirk he fought a battle at the end of a campaign which had the hallmark of genius. He lured Edward forward to the point where that king, the epitome of the military virtues, was almost defeated without the need for battle. When an engagement became unavoidable, Wallace's dispositions so blunted the English attacks that it required the defection of the Scottish cavalry, upon which he relied to counter the English archers, to give Edward the opening which led to victory. Self-taught, Wallace was adept not merely in the small action but also, in the context of the pitched battle, as both Stirling and Falkirk demonstrated, a master of training and motivation. The thousands who stood and died at Falkirk were testimony to his powers.

The connection between Wallace's methods and those of Bruce is a direct one if not unbroken. Whether Bruce was a close ally of Wallace or in any way sympathetic to him is open to doubt; given Bruce's opposition to the Balliol cause, it is unlikely. Bruce was not present at Stirling, and his part at Falkirk is still unclear. He cannot have seen Wallace as an equal. But that he learned from him emerges from his campaigns after Methven. There, he neglected the lesson which Wallace had taught. Methven was in a sense Bruce clinging to the old and tried but futile kind of war which was in his blood. Had he defeated Aymer de Valence there, he would have had no cause to alter his tactics; ultimately, faced by Edward, he would have perished. He was forced to adapt because of the defeat at Methven, and it was to the example of Wallace that he turned. He perfected Wallace's tactics, and if this is true of the minor engagement, of the raid and the ambush, it is no less true of Bannockburn. The paramount need for training, the choice of site, the importance of a single command which Bruce enjoyed as Wallace could not, these were the lessons which he put into effect at Bannockburn. Bruce, with the authority of kingship, had the use of a cavalry force as Wallace did not. It was that use which allowed him to follow Wallace's intention and rout the English archers. That done, his victory over Edward II was easier to achieve.

The man who had failed in his twin ambitions did not fail in the legacy he left to his countrymen. Wallace taught the Scots that within each of them lay his own destiny. From him a people defeated and downtrodden, distrustful (with good reason) of its leaders, learned anew that spirit of defiant unity which alone could bring independence. With the advantage of hindsight we can see that Wallace was over-ambitious, that the task he had taken upon himself was too great for him or for any individual. He had to face an implacable enemy in Edward I who could call up against him an overwhelming superiority of numbers. In the Scottish nobles he had to deal with a group which, if not actively hostile, was suspicious of him and unreliable. He had to educate the people from whom he had come, to accept their own potential and to put it to the test. He had to do this without wealth or position. He was denied the time and the resources necessary for any hope of success. In his violence and cruelty he was a man of his time. In his aspirations and in the breadth of his vision he stepped outside that time. We have no contemporary picture of him; we need none. In his cry at Westminster that he was no traitor we can see him far more accurately and far more truly than in any picture. Wallace was no traitor to Edward, for he had given him no oath of allegiance. He was no traitor to Balliol, for he died for him. Most important of all, he was no traitor to himself, for he had never deviated from that personal code of honour which he had adopted after Lanark. If it was peculiar to him, it made him what he was. And it is for what he was that he is best and most properly remembered.

Select Bibliography

Introductory Note

We lack any contemporary Scottish accounts of the life of William Wallace. By far the best-known life is that by Henry the Minstrel or Blind Harry which, however prejudiced and inaccurate, carries on that adulatory attitude towards the Guardian which first appears in John of Fordun, who died about 1385, eighty years after Wallace's execution. Fordun cannot wholly be discounted for he is the nearest source we have to Wallace's own time, and it is not unreasonable to assume, therefore, that he had recourse to material which has since disappeared. Fordun in turn was drawn on by the likes of Andrew of Wyntoun, the author of a chronicle of about 1420, and Walter Bower, whose *Scotichronicon* was written twenty years after Wyntoun. Both Wyntoun and Bower, whose work was, essentially, an amplification of Fordun, shared the latter's intention. They were concerned with politics and propaganda, with England the enemy as in Wallace's own day. Some thirty years after Bower, Blind Harry produced his account, fiercely anti-English and, as shown by Mr. M. McDiarmid, unreliable for the serious student of history. The impact of the book on the popular imagination, particularly in the version in modern English by William Hamilton of Gilberton, cannot be ignored and lasts to this day, however. John Major or Mair, who died in 1550, while not entirely free of the tradition to which his predecessors subscribed, looked more to the future than they, and saw the virtue, which they would have scorned, of an eventual union between Scotland and England.

Bain, J. (ed.): *Calendar of Documents relating to Scotland, 1108-1509*. Edinburgh, 1881-4.

Barbour, John: see Mackenzie, W.M.

Barron, E.M: *The Scottish War of Independence*. Inverness, 1934.

Barrow, G.W.S: *The Kingdom of the Scots*. London, 1973. *Robert Bruce & the Community of the Realm of Scotland*. Edinburgh, 1976. 'Lothian in the First War of Independence, 1296-1328', *S.H.R. LV*, 2, no. 160, Oct. 1976, pp. 151-171. *The Anglo-Norman Era in Scottish History*. Oxford, 1980. *Kingship & Unity, Scotland 1100-1306*. London, 1981.

Bellamy, J.G: *The Law of Treason in England in the Later Middle Ages*. Cambridge, 1970.

Bower, Walter: see Goodall, W.

Brown, P.H: *History of Scotland*. Cambridge, 1911.

Brie, F.W.D. (ed.): *The Brut, or the Chronicles of England*. London, 1908.

Calendar of the Close Rolls preserved in the Public Record Office.

Calendar of the Close Rolls preserved in the Public Record Office.

Calendar of Documents relating to Scotland, 1108-1509: see Bain, J.

Chronicles of the Reigns of Edward I and Edward II: see Stubbs, W.

von Clausewitz, C: *On War* (ed. & trans. by M. Howard & P. Paret). Princeton, 1984.

Cotton, Bartholomew: see Luard, H.R.

Denholm-Young, N. (ed.): *Vita Edwardi Secundi*. Edinburgh, 1957.

Dickinson, W.C., Donaldson, G., Milne, I.A: *A Source Book of Scottish History*. Vol. 1. London, 1952.

Dictionary of National Biography.

Documents Illustrative of the History of Scotland: see Stevenson, J.

Dodgshon, R: *Land and Society in Early Scotland*. Oxford, 1981.

Donaldson, G: *Scottish Historical Documents*. Edinburgh, 1974.

Duncan, A.A.M: *The Nation of Scots*. London, 1970 (Historical Association Pamphlet)

English Historical Review (*E.H.R*).

Ferguson, W: *Scotland's Relations with England: a Survey to 1707*. Edinburgh, 1977.

Fergusson, J: *William Wallace, Guardian of Scotland*. London, 1938.

Fordun, John of: see Skene, W.F.

Goodall, W. (ed.): *Scotichronicron cum Continuatione Walteri Boweri*. Edinburgh, 1759.

Gray, sir Thomas: see Maxwell, H.

Guisborough, Walter of: see Rothwell, H.

Hamilton, W: *The History of the Life and Adventures and Heroic Actions of the Renowned Sir William Wallace*. Edinburgh, 1816.

Harry, Blind (Henry the Minstrel): see McDiarmid, M.P.

Hog, T. (ed.): *Nicholas Trivet: Annales*. London, 1845.

Keen, M.H: *The Laws of War in the Late Middle Ages*. London, 1965. *The Outlaws of Medieval Legend*. London, 1961. 'Treason Trials under the Law of Arms'. *E.H.R.*, 5th Series, xii, 1962.

Kightly, C: *Folk Heroes of Britain*. London, 1982.

Laing, D. (ed.): *The Oryginale Cronykil of Scotland, by Andrew of Wyntoun*. Edinburgh, 1879.

Lanercost, Chronicle of: see Maxwell, H.

Lang, A: *History of Scotland*. 4 vols. Edinburgh, 1903-7.

Langtoft, Peter of: see Wright, T.

Luard, H.R. (ed.): *Bartholomew Cotton, Historia Anglicana*. London, 1859.

Matthew of Westminster, *Flores Historiarum*, 3 vols. London, 1890.

McDiarmid, M.P. (ed.): *Blind Harry: Wallace*. 2 vols. Edinburgh, 1968-9.

Machiavelli, N: *The Art of War*. Revised edition of the Ellis Farneworth translation. New York, 1965.

MacKay, J.A: *Robert Bruce, King of Scots*. London, 1974.

Mackenzie, A.M: *Robert Bruce, King of Scots*. Edinburgh, 1934.

Mackenzie, W.M. (ed.): *John Barbour: the Bruce*. London 1909.

Mackie, J.D: *A History of Scotland*. Edinburgh, 1964.

Macpherson, D. (ed.): *Rotuli Scotiae, 1291-1516*. 2 vols. London, 1814 & 1819.

Major, John: *Historia Majoris Britanniae*. Edinburgh, 1740.

Maxwell, H. (ed. & trans.): *Chronicle of Lanercost*. Glasgow, 1913. *Sir Thomas Gray: Scalacronicon*. Glasgow, 1907.

Morris, J.E: *The Welsh Wars of Edward I*. Oxford, 1901. 'Mounted Infantry in Medieval Warfare'. R.H.S. 3rd Series, Vol. VIII. 1914.

Murison, A.F: *Sir William Wallace*. London, 1898.

Nicholson, R: *Scotland: the Later Middle Ages*. Edinburgh, 1974.

Oman, C.W.C: *The Art of War in the Middle Ages, 1378-1515*. New York, 1960.

Palgrave, F. (ed.): *Parliamentary Writs and Writs of Summons, Edward I and Edward II*. 2 vols. London, 1827-34.

Palgrave, F. (ed.): *Documents and Records Illustrating the History of Scotland, 1237-1307*. London, 1837.

Plucknett, T.F.T: *Edward I and the Criminal Law*. Cambridge, 1960. *A Concise History of the Common Law*. London, 1956.

Pluscardensis, Liber: see Skene, F.H.J.

Political Songs of England: see Wright, T.

Powicke, F.M: *The Thirteenth Century, 1216-1307*. Oxford, 1953.

Prestwich, M: *The Three Edwards, War and State in England, 1272-1377*. London, 1981.

Ramsay, J: *The Dawn of the Constitution, 1216-1307*. London, 1908.

Reid, N: 'The Kingless Kingdom: the Scottish Guardianship of 1286-1306', *S.H.R.*, *LXI*, 2, no. 172, 1982.

Riley, H.T. (ed.): *William Rishanger: Chronica et Annales*. London, 1865.

Rishanger: see Riley.

Ritchie, R.L.G: *The Normans in Scotland*. Edinburgh, 1953.

Rothwell, H. (ed.): *Chronicle of Walter of Guisborough*. London, 1957.

Rotuli Scotiae: see Macpherson, D.

Rymer, T. (ed.): *Foedera*. London, 1816-30.

Salzman, F: *Edward I*. London, 1968.

Scalacronicon: see Maxwell, H.

Scotichronicon: see Skene, W.F.

Scottish Historical Review(S.H.R.).

Skene, F.H.J. (ed.): *Liber Pluscardensis*. Edinburgh, 1880.

Skene, W.F. (ed.): *John of Fordun: Scotichronicon* (trans. F.S.H. Skene). 2 vols. Edinburgh, 1871-2.

Stevenson, J. (ed.): *Documents Illustrative of the History of Scotland, 1286-1306*. Edinburgh, 1870. *Documents illustrative of Sir William Wallace, his life and time*. Edinburgh, 1841.

Stones, E.L.G. (ed.): *Anglo-Scottish Relations, 1174-1328. Some Selected Documents*. Edinburgh, 1964.

Stones, E.L.G. and Simpson, G.G: *Edward I and the Throne of Scotland, 1290-6*. 2 vols. Oxford, 1979.

Stones, E.L.G: *Edward I*. Oxford, 1968.

Stubbs, W. (ed.): *Chronicles of the Reigns of Edward I and Edward II*, 2 vols. London, 1882-3.

Tout, T.F: *Chapters in the Administrative History of Medieval England*. Manchester, 1920-33.

Trivét, Nicholas: see Hog, T.

Vickers, K.H: *England in the later Middle Ages*. London, 1961.

Warren, W.L: *Henry II*. London, 1983.

Westminster, Matthew of: see Luard, H.R.

Wright, T. (ed.): *Peter of Langtoft: Metrical Chronicle*. London, 1866. *Political Songs of England*. London, 1839.

Wyntoun, Andrew of: see Laing, D.

Index

143